Woman'sDay

Christmas Cookies
Candies & Cakes

Woman'sDay

Christmas Cookies
Candies & Cakes

filipacchi publishing

Contents

Peppermint Sticks

MAKES 48 · PREP AND CHILL: 3 HR · BAKE: 11 TO 13 MIN PER BATCH
DECORATE: ABOUT 20 MIN

2 sticks (1 cup) unsalted butter, softened

1 cup granulated sugar

½ tsp each vanilla extract and salt

2 large eggs

2¾ cups all-purpose flour

2 tsp mint extract

12 drops each green and red food color

1 cup white chocolate chips

12 each green and red peppermint candies, crushed

Storage tip: Store airtight at cool room temperature up to 1 week.

1 In a large bowl with mixer on medium speed, beat butter, sugar, vanilla and salt until fluffy. Beat in eggs, 1 at a time. On low speed, gradually add flour; beat just until blended. Divide dough in half. Shape half into a 6-in. disk; wrap and refrigerate. Stir mint extract into other half; divide that half in half. Stir green food color into 1 half, red into the other (colors will be pale). Shape each into a 5-in. disk; wrap separately and refrigerate 2 hours or until firm.

2 Heat oven to 350°F. Have baking sheet(s) ready.

3 Cut uncolored dough in 12 equal wedges and each disk tinted dough in 6 equal wedges.

4 On a lightly floured surface, roll 1 uncolored wedge and 1 tinted wedge into 15-in.-long ropes (keep rest of dough refrigerated). Place ropes side by side; cut crosswise in quarters. Holding ends of both ropes, twist together from 1 end to the other (handle gently; dough is soft). Place 1 in. apart on ungreased baking sheet(s). Repeat with remaining dough.

5 Bake 11 to 13 minutes until edges are lightly browned. Remove to racks to cool.

6 To decorate: Melt chocolate chips as package directs. Dip about ½ in. of both ends of each cookie in chocolate, letting excess drip off, then dip in crushed candies. Place on wax paper until chocolate sets.

PER STICK: 107 cal, 1 g pro, 14 g car, 0 g fiber, 5 g fat (3 g sat fat), 20 mg chol, 32 mg sod

Chocolate, Cherry & Pistachio Pinwheels

**MAKES ABOUT 40 · PREP AND FREEZE: ABOUT 2¼ HR
BAKE: 10 TO 12 MIN PER BATCH**

1½ sticks (¾ cup) unsalted butter, softened

1 cup granulated sugar

1 tsp baking powder

½ tsp salt

1 large egg plus yolk of 1 large egg

2 cups all-purpose flour

1 oz unsweetened baking chocolate, melted and cooled as pkg directs

1 tsp vanilla extract

¼ cup shelled pistachio nuts, finely chopped

½ tsp almond extract

8 drops each green and red food color

¼ cup dried sweetened cherries or cranberries, finely chopped

1 Beat butter, sugar, baking powder and salt in a large bowl with mixer on high speed 3 minutes or until fluffy. Beat in egg and yolk until well blended. Reduce mixer speed to low; beat in flour just until combined.

2 Divide dough in thirds; place each portion in a separate bowl. Add melted chocolate and ½ tsp vanilla extract to 1 bowl; pistachios, almond extract and green food color to another bowl; and cherries, remaining ½ tsp vanilla extract and red food color to the last bowl. Stir each until ingredients are blended.

3 Place each portion between 2 sheets of wax paper. With a rolling pin, roll each into a 10 x 8-in. rectangle. Remove top sheets of paper. Invert cherry layer on chocolate layer, remove wax paper, then invert pistachio layer on cherry layer. Freeze 10 minutes until slightly firm. Remove wax paper from top. Starting at a long side, tightly roll up jelly-roll style, peeling off bottom sheet of wax paper as you go and pressing together any cracks in chocolate dough. Wrap and freeze 45 minutes until firm enough to slice.

4 Heat oven to 350°F. Have baking sheet(s) ready. Cut log in ¼-in.-thick slices. Place pinwheels 2 in. apart on ungreased baking sheet(s).

5 Bake 10 to 12 minutes until bottoms are light golden. Immediately remove to a wire rack to cool completely.

PER COOKIE: 87 cal, 1 g pro, 11 g car, 0 g fiber, 4 g fat (3 g sat fat), 19 mg chol, 69 mg sod

Storage tip: Store airtight at room temperature up to 1 week, or freeze up to 1 month.

Almond Biscotti

2 large eggs

½ cup granulated sugar

½ cup oil

1 Tbsp anise extract

1½ tsp baking powder

1½ cups all-purpose flour

¾ cup sliced almonds, toasted

Decoration: confectioners' sugar

Storage tip: Store airtight at cool room temperature up to 2 weeks, or freeze up to 2 months.

1 Heat oven to 350°F. Coat a baking sheet with cooking spray.

2 Vigorously whisk eggs, sugar, oil and extract in a large bowl until blended. Stir in baking powder, then flour until combined. Stir in almonds.

3 Spoon ⅓ dough onto a prepared baking sheet. With floured hands (dough will be soft and sticky) form dough into an 11-in.-long, 2-in.-wide strip. Repeat with remaining dough, making 2 more strips. Place about 1½ in. apart on the baking sheet.

4 Bake 20 to 23 minutes or until firm and bottoms are golden. Cool on baking sheet on a wire rack 5 minutes, then transfer to a cutting board. Using a sharp serrated knife, slice strips diagonally into ½-in. thick slices. Lay slices flat on baking sheet(s).

5 Bake 12 to 15 minutes, turning biscotti over halfway through baking, until lightly toasted. Transfer to a wire rack to cool. If desired, dust with confectioners' sugar before serving.

PER COOKIE: 46 cal, 1 g pro, 5 g car, 0 g fiber, 3 g fat (0 g sat fat), 7 mg chol, 16 mg sod

Chocolate-Coconut Rugelach

MAKES 48 · PREP & CHILL: 6½ HR · BAKE: 18 TO 22 MIN PER BATCH

CREAM CHEESE PASTRY

2 sticks (1 cup) unsalted butter, softened

1 brick (8 oz) cream cheese, softened

¼ cup granulated sugar

2 cups all-purpose flour

⅓ cup fig preserves

1½ cups sweetened shredded coconut

½ cup semisweet chocolate mini-chips

4 Tbsp granulated sugar

Decoration: white coarse (crystal) sugar

Storage tip: Store airtight with wax paper between layers at cool room temperature up to 1 week, or freeze up to 3 months.

---

1 Cream Cheese Pastry: Beat butter and cream cheese in a large bowl with mixer on medium speed until well combined. On low speed, beat in sugar and flour until blended.

2 Divide dough in quarters. Shape each portion into a 1-in.-thick disk. Wrap individually; refrigerate at least 4 hours until firm enough to roll out.

3 Heat oven to 350°F. Place oven rack in upper third of oven.

4 Melt preserves in microwave or a saucepan over low heat (strain if chunky).

5 On floured surface, roll 1 disk into a 10-in. circle. Brush with a quarter of the preserves (it will barely cover dough). Sprinkle with 6 Tbsp coconut, 2 Tbsp chocolate chips and 1 Tbsp granulated sugar. Gently press so fillings adhere to dough. With a pizza wheel or knife, cut circle in 12 wedges. Roll up from wide edge to point. Place 2 in. apart on ungreased baking sheet(s); sprinkle wedges with coarse sugar.

6 Bake in upper third of oven 18 to 22 minutes or until golden brown. Remove to a wire rack to cool. Repeat with remaining dough and filling.

PER COOKIE: 113 cal, 1 g pro, 12 g car, 0 g fiber, 7 g fat (5 g sat fat), 15 mg chol, 23 mg sod

SHAPED COOKIES

St. Joseph's Day Fig Cookies

MAKES 48 · PREP & CHILL: 2 HR · BAKE: 14 TO 19 MIN PER BATCH
DECORATE: ABOUT 15 MIN

FILLING

2 cups (12 oz) coarsely chopped, trimmed dried figs

1 cup (6 oz) coarsely chopped dried dates

Generous ½ cup orange marmalade

1 tsp freshly grated orange zest

3 Tbsp orange juice, plus more if needed

2 Tbsp unsalted butter, melted

1½ tsp ground cinnamon

DOUGH

3 cups all-purpose flour

Generous ¼ cup granulated sugar

½ tsp baking powder

¼ tsp salt

1 cup solid vegetable shortening

ICING

1¼ cups confectioners' sugar

2 Tbsp milk, plus more if needed

¼ tsp anise extract or ½ tsp vanilla extract

1 drop each red and green food color

Decoration: multicolored nonpareils

1 **Filling:** Process ingredients in a food processor until coarsely puréed. If dry, add about 1 Tbsp more juice. (Can be refrigerated up to 4 days. Bring to room temperature and stir before using.)

2 **Dough:** In food processor, pulse flour, sugar, baking powder and salt to mix. Drop spoonfuls shortening over mixture; pulse until coarse crumbs form. Sprinkle with ⅓ cup plus 1½ Tbsp ice water; pulse just until evenly moistened. Place dough on wax paper; knead until a smooth, slightly moist (not wet) dough forms. If dry or crumbly, knead in 1 to 2 tsp water.

3 Divide in half. Place each portion between sheets of wax paper. Roll each into a 12-in. square, cutting and patching to even sides. Stack (paper attached) on a baking sheet. Refrigerate 30 minutes until cold and firm.

4 Position racks to divide oven in thirds. Heat oven to 375°F.

5 Working with 1 portion (leave rest refrigerated), gently peel away 1 sheet of wax paper, then lightly pat back into place. Flip dough over on work surface; peel off top sheet. Cut dough crosswise into four 12 x 3-in. strips. Spoon about ⅓ cup filling down middle of each. Fold over about 1 in. on each side to cover filling. Moisten edges, overlap slightly; press seams to seal. Trim uneven ends. Cut strips crosswise in 2-in. pieces. Place seam side down, 2 in. apart, on ungreased baking sheet(s). Cut 2 parallel 1-in. slits down each cookie to expose filling. Slightly bend in crescent shapes. Repeat with remaining dough and remaining filling.

6 Bake 1 sheet at a time in upper third of oven 14 to 19 minutes until slightly darker at edges, reversing sheet from front to back halfway through baking. Cool on sheet on a

PER COOKIE: 125 cal, 1 g pro, 21 g car, 1 g fiber, 4 g fat (1 g sat fat), 1 mg chol, 48 mg sod

wire rack 1 to 2 minutes before transferring cookies to rack to cool completely.

7 Icing: Stir ingredients in a medium bowl to form a fluid icing; add more milk if needed. Transfer ⅓ to a small bowl; stir in red food color. Transfer half of remaining icing to another small bowl; stir in green color.

8 Set racks with cookies on wax paper. Using a spoon, drizzle a line of pink icing crosswise over cookies, sprinkling with nonpareils before icing sets. Keeping colors separated, neatly drizzle lines of green and white icing over cookies, sprinkling with more nonpareils. Let stand 1 hour or until icing completely sets.

SHAPED COOKIES

Stained Glass Cookies

MAKES 12 TREES AND 12 ROUND COOKIES · PREP & CHILL: 1 HR
BAKE: 8 TO 10 MIN PER BATCH

10 Tbsp plus 2 tsp (⅔ cup) unsalted butter, softened

1 cup granulated sugar

1 tsp baking powder

½ tsp salt

1 large egg

1 tsp vanilla extract

2 cups plus 2 Tbsp all-purpose flour

3 rolls (1.14 oz each) regular five-flavors-a-roll Life Savers candies, each color crushed separately

You also need: 6¼- and 3¼-in. Christmas tree cookie cutters and 3- and 1½-in. round cookie cutters

1 Beat butter, sugar, baking powder and salt in a large bowl with mixer on medium speed 3 minutes or until fluffy. Beat in egg and vanilla until well blended.

2 On low speed, gradually beat in flour until just blended. Divide dough in half, shape each into a 1-in.-thick disk and wrap separately. Refrigerate 30 minutes or up to four days (warm slightly before using).

3 Heat oven to 350°F. Line baking sheet(s) with foil; coat with cooking spray. Have cookie cutters ready.

4 On lightly floured surface, with floured rolling pin, roll out 1 disk dough (keep other refrigerated) to ¼ in. thick. Use large cutter to cut out trees. Place 2 in. apart on lined baking sheet(s). Use small tree cutter to cut a "window" in center of each. Repeat with round cutters. Reroll and cut scraps once.

5 Bake one sheet at a time 6 to 8 minutes or until just barely tinged brown at edges. Using a drinking straw, punch out holes on sides of trees as shown (ornaments) and hanging holes on top of cookies, if desired. Using a small spoon, fill cutouts, except hanging holes, with candy until level with top of dough. Brush off stray bits. Bake 4 minutes or until candy melts.

6 Cool on sheets on wire rack 7 to 10 minutes until "glass" cools and hardens. Transfer cookies with a broad metal spatula to wire rack to cool completely.

7 To display cookies, hang in a window or on a Christmas tree.

PER COOKIE: 137 cal, 1 g pro, 21 g car, 0 g fiber, 5 g fat (3 g sat fat), 22 mg chol, 77 mg sod

Angel Wings

MAKES 48 · PREP & CHILL: 4¾ HR · BAKE: 8 TO 10 MIN PER BATCH

1 stick (½ cup) unsalted butter, softened

1 cup granulated sugar

2 tsp baking powder

1 large egg

½ tsp pure almond extract

1⅔ cups all-purpose flour

¼ cup cornstarch

Decoration: white of 1 large egg, slightly beaten, sliced almonds and sugar

1 Beat butter, sugar and baking powder in a large bowl with mixer on low speed to blend. Increase to medium-high and beat until fluffy. Beat in egg and almond extract. On low speed, beat in flour and cornstarch until just blended.

2 Divide dough in half. Shape each portion into a 1-in.-thick disk. Wrap individually and refrigerate at least 4 hours or until firm enough to roll out.

3 Heat oven to 350°F. Have ready a 2½-in. heart-shaped cookie cutter.

4 On lightly floured wax paper with lightly floured rolling pin, roll 1 disk (keep other refrigerated) to ⅛ in. thick. Cut out hearts with cookie cutter. Slide paper onto a baking sheet; freeze 5 to 10 minutes or until firm and easy to handle.

5 Peel hearts off paper. Place 1 in. apart on ungreased baking sheet. Cut a 1½-in.-long slit at bottom of hearts. Spread apart slightly to form wings. Brush hearts with egg white. Attach almonds as shown, pressing down gently. Sprinkle with a little sugar. (Reroll scraps only once or cookies will be tough.)

6 Bake 8 to 10 minutes until just golden brown at edges. Remove to wire rack to cool. Repeat with remaining dough.

PER COOKIE: 83 cal, 1 g pro, 11 g car, 1 g fiber, 4 g fat (1 g sat fat), 9 mg chol, 39 mg sod

Gingerbread Kids

MAKES 7 LARGE, 30 SMALL · PREP & CHILL: ABOUT 6¾ HR
BAKE: 13 TO 19 MIN PER BATCH · DECORATE: ABOUT 30 MIN

5½ cups all-purpose flour

1½ Tbsp ground ginger

2 tsp ground cinnamon

1 tsp baking powder

½ tsp each ground cloves and nutmeg

½ tsp salt

¼ tsp baking soda

2 sticks (1 cup) unsalted butter, softened

1 cup light molasses

½ cup each granulated sugar and packed brown sugar

2 large eggs

2 tsp vanilla extract

2 Tbsp cider vinegar

1 cup Sugar in the Raw or coarse white decorating sugar

Decorating Icing
(recipe follows)

You also need: 8-in. and 4-in. gingerbread boy cookie cutters; pastry bag fitted with small basket-weave tip; small ziptop bags (for small cookies); black and pink jelly beans; red hearts candy; red nonpareils; cinnamon drop candies; and blue, pink and yellow candy flower decors

1 Whisk flour, ginger, cinnamon, baking powder, cloves, nutmeg, salt and baking soda in a bowl to blend.

2 Beat butter, molasses, sugars, eggs, vanilla and vinegar in a large bowl with mixer on medium speed to blend. On low speed, beat in flour mixture, 1 cup at a time, until a soft dough forms. Divide in thirds. Shape each third on plastic wrap into a 1-in.-thick disk. Wrap; chill 4 hours until firm.

3 Lightly dust 1 disk at a time with flour (keep others chilled). Roll out between sheets of plastic wrap to ¼ in. thick for large cookies, ⅛ in. thick for small. Slide onto a baking sheet; freeze at least 15 minutes. Repeat with rest of dough, stacking sheets in freezer. Reroll scraps and cut once. Peel off top plastic wrap. Using floured cookie cutters, cut out cookies, leave on plastic and slide back on baking sheet. Freeze 10 minutes.

4 Heat oven to 350°F. Line baking sheet(s) with nonstick foil.

5 Place cookies 1 in. apart on lined baking sheet(s). Sprinkle with sugar.

6 Bake 17 to 19 minutes for large cookies, 13 to 15 minutes for small, until a bit darker. Cool slightly on sheet on a wire rack; move to rack to cool completely.

7 To decorate: Fill basket-weave–tipped pastry bag with icing. Cut jelly beans in half. Small cookies: Using icing as glue, glue on blue candy flower eyes, cinnamon drop buttons. Using ziptop bag of icing, pipe on rickrack trim, hair and smiles. Large cookies (not shown): Glue on jelly-bean eyes, noses and cheeks and candy-heart buttons.

Note: Find Just Whites in the baking section of your supermarket or in stores selling cake-decorating supplies.

Pipe rickrack trim; sprinkle with nonpareils. Fill a small ziptop bag with icing, snip tip off corner and pipe hair; sprinkle with nonpareils. Pipe on smiles. For girls, glue candy flower decors on hair. Let dry at least 6 hours.

DECORATING ICING Beat 1 lb confectioners' sugar (3¼ cups) and ¼ cup Just Whites (powdered egg whites, see Note) in a large bowl with mixer on low speed until combined. Add ⅓ cup water; beat until blended. Increase speed to high; beat 8 minutes or until icing is very thick and white. Makes 2½ cups.

PER LARGE COOKIE: 393 cal, 5 g pro, 74 g car, 1 g fiber, 9 g fat (5 g sat fat), 41 mg chol, 124 mg sod

PER SMALL COOKIE: 197 cal, 2 g pro, 37 g car, 0 g fiber, 5 g fat (3 g sat fat), 21 mg chol, 62 mg sod

Storage tip: Store airtight in a single layer at cool room temperature up to 2 weeks, or freeze up to 3 months.

Spice-Cookie Snowmen

MAKES 56 · PREP & CHILL: 1½ HR · BAKE: 8 TO 10 MIN · DECORATE: 1 HR

3 sticks (1½ cups) unsalted butter, softened

1 cup granulated sugar

1 large egg

1 tsp vanilla extract

1½ tsp ground cinnamon

1 tsp ground ginger

¼ tsp each ground allspice and cloves

¼ tsp salt

4 cups all-purpose flour

DECORATING ICING
(Makes 2½ cups)

1 lb confectioners' sugar (3¼ cups)

3 Tbsp Just Whites (powdered egg whites, see Note)

6 Tbsp water

You also need: 4-in. snowman cookie cutter with arms and legs; red, green and black paste food colors; fine white decorating (crystal) sugar (see Note); orange sprinkles (jimmies); and small ziptop bags

1 Beat butter and sugar in a large bowl with mixer on low speed until fluffy. Beat in egg, vanilla, spices and salt. On low speed, beat in flour until just blended.

2 Gather dough together and divide in thirds. Shape each portion into a 1-in.-thick disk and wrap separately. Chill 1 hour or until firm.

3 Heat oven to 375°F. Have baking sheet(s) ready.

4 On floured surface with floured rolling pin, roll out 1 disk at a time (keep rest refrigerated) to ¼ in. thick. Using floured cookie cutter, cut out snowmen. Place 1 in. apart on ungreased baking sheet(s). Reroll and cut scraps once.

5 Bake 8 to 10 minutes or until bottoms and edges are just brown. Cool on sheet on a wire rack 2 minutes before removing to rack to cool completely.

6 Decorating Icing: In a large bowl, with mixer on low speed, beat confectioners' sugar and Just Whites until combined. Add water; beat until blended. Increase mixer speed to high and beat 8 minutes or until icing is very thick and white.

7 To ice and decorate: For each color, put a small portion of Decorating Icing into a cup. Stir in food color. Leave remaining icing white.

SHAPED COOKIES

Note: Find paste food colors, decorating sugar and Just Whites in the baking section of your supermarket or in stores selling cake-decorating supplies.

8 Spoon some white icing into a ziptop bag. Cut tip off a corner; pipe outline on areas of snowman that will be white. To thin icing for coating: Add drops of water to white icing in bowl until thin enough to spread without dripping. Dip a brush into thinned white icing. Spread to piped border; sprinkle hands and feet with decorating sugar. Let dry 3 hours.

9 Put colored icing into bags, cut a corner off each bag; pipe in hats and scarves. Thin remaining colored icing; fill in. Pipe buttons and eyes and insert orange sprinkles as noses. Let dry at least 6 hours before storing in a single layer.

PER COOKIE: 124 cal, 1 g pro, 19 g car, 0 g fiber, 5 g fat (3 g sat fat), 17 mg chol, 17 mg sod

Sugar-Cookie Cutouts

MAKES ABOUT 36 · PREP: 30 MIN · BAKE: 6 TO 7 MIN PER BATCH

2¾ cups all-purpose flour

2 tsp baking powder

1 tsp salt

2 sticks (1 cup) unsalted butter, softened

1½ cups granulated sugar

1 egg

1½ tsp vanilla extract

½ tsp almond extract

1 Heat oven to 400º F. In medium bowl, combine flour, baking powder and salt. In large bowl with electric mixer, beat butter and sugar until light and fluffy. Beat in egg and extracts. Add flour mixture to butter mixture, 1 cup at a time, mixing after each addition, until blended. Do not chill dough.

2 Divide dough into 2 balls. On a floured surface with a floured rolling pin, roll each ball into a circle approximately 12 in. in diameter and ⅛-in. thick. Dip cookie cutter in flour before each use. Place cookies 1 in. apart on ungreased baking sheets. Bake 6 to 7 minutes or until cookies are lightly browned.

3 Cool in pan on wire rack for 2 minutes. Remove to rack to cool completely. Decorate as desired with prepared frosting and icing.

PER COOKIE: 115 cal, 1 g pro, 16 g car, 0 g fiber, 5 g fat (3 g sat fat), 19 mg chol, 99 mg sod

CARROT CUTOUTS

Add ½ tsp each ground cinnamon, ground nutmeg and ground cloves to flour mixture. Add 1½ cups finely grated carrots and, if desired, ½ cup finely chopped walnuts to cookie dough with flour mixture.

PER COOKIE: 117 cal, 1 g pro, 16 g car, 0 g fiber, 5 g fat (3 g sat fat), 19 mg chol, 101 mg sod

LEMON CUTOUTS

Substitute ½ tsp lemon extract for almond extract. Stir 3 Tbsp lemon zest (about 3 lemons) into cookie dough with flour mixture.

PER COOKIE: 115 cal, 1 g pro, 16 g car, 0 g fiber, 5 g fat (3 g sat fat), 19 mg chol, 99 mg sod

CHOCOLATE-ORANGE CUTOUTS

Add 3 squares (3 oz) unsweetened chocolate, melted and cooled, to butter mixture before adding flour mixture. Stir 2 Tbsp grated orange zest into cookie dough with flour mixture.

PER COOKIE: 127 cal, 2 g pro, 17 g car, 1 g fiber, 7 g fat (4 g sat fat), 19 mg chol, 99 mg sod

COCONUT CUTOUTS

Add 1 cup sweetened shredded coconut, toasted and finely chopped, to cookie dough with flour mixture.

PER COOKIE: 128 cal, 1 g pro, 17 g car, 0 g fiber, 6 g fat (4 g sat fat), 19 mg chol, 105 mg sod

PEPPERMINT CUTOUTS

Add ⅓ cup peppermint crunch sprinkles or finely crushed peppermint candies to cookie dough with flour mixture.

PER COOKIE: 125 cal, 1 g pro, 18 g car, 0 g fiber, 5 g fat (3 g sat fat), 19 mg chol, 98 mg sod

Spice-Cookie Cutouts

MAKES 50 3-IN. COOKIES · PREP & CHILL: ABOUT 1½ HR
BAKE: 10 TO 12 MIN PER BATCH

3 sticks (1½ cups) unsalted butter, softened

1 cup granulated sugar

1 large egg, at room temperature

1 tsp vanilla extract

1½ tsp ground cinnamon

1 tsp ground ginger

¼ tsp each ground allspice and cloves

¼ tsp salt

4 cups all-purpose flour

DECORATING ICING
(Makes 2½ cups)

1 lb confectioners' sugar (3¼ cups)

3 Tbsp Just Whites (powdered egg whites, see Note)

6 Tbsp water

You also need: assorted snowflake cookie cutters, ziptop bags, small paintbrushes, white sanding (fine crystal) or granulated sugar

Note: Find Just Whites in the baking section of your supermarket or in stores selling cake-decorating supplies.

1 Beat butter and sugar in a large bowl with mixer on high speed until pale and fluffy. Beat in egg, vanilla, spices and salt. On low, beat in flour until just blended.

2 Shape dough into three 1-in.-thick disks. Wrap each and chill 1 hour or until firm.

3 Heat oven to 375°F.

4 On floured surface, with floured rolling pin, roll out 1 disk at a time (keep rest refrigerated) to ¼ in. thick. Cut out desired shapes with floured cookie cutters. Place 1 in. apart on ungreased baking sheet(s). Reroll scraps.

5 Bake 10 to 12 minutes until bottoms and edges are just brown. Cool on sheet on a wire rack 3 minutes before removing to rack to cool completely.

6 Decorating Icing: In a large bowl, with mixer on low speed, beat confectioners' sugar and Just Whites until combined. Add water; beat until blended. Increase mixer speed to high and beat 8 minutes or until icing is very thick and white.

7 To ice and decorate Snowflakes: Pipe white designs; let dry. Sprinkle with sugar; gently shake off excess.

8 To coat: Dip a brush into thinned icing. Spread to piped border. Let set 3 hours.

PER COOKIE: 141 cal, 2 g pro, 21 g car, 0 g fiber, 5 g fat (3 g sat fat), 19 mg chol, 14 mg sod

Pecan-Jam Stars

MAKES 50 · PREP & CHILL: ABOUT 1 HR 10 MIN · BAKE: 8 TO 10 MIN PER BATCH

2/3 cup pecan halves

3 cups all-purpose flour

1/2 tsp salt

3 sticks (1 1/2 cups) unsalted butter, softened

1 1/4 cups confectioners' sugar, plus extra for dusting

2 1/2 tsp vanilla extract

1/2 cup each seedless red raspberry jam and apricot jam

You also need: *2-in. and 1-in. star cookie cutters*

Storage tip: Store filled cookies airtight in a single layer; refrigerate up to 1 week. Unfilled, freeze up to 3 months.

1 Heat oven to 350°F. Toast nuts 5 to 7 minutes until fragrant. Cool completely. Leave open heating.

2 Pulse nuts and 1/4 cup flour in food processor until nuts are finely ground. Whisk nut mixture, remaining flour and salt in a bowl to combine.

3 Beat butter, sugar and vanilla in a large bowl with mixer on medium speed to blend. On low speed, beat in flour mixture. Divide dough in fourths; roll each portion between sheets of wax paper to 1/8 in. thick. Slide dough onto baking sheets, stacking sheets of dough. Chill 30 minutes or until firm.

4 Peel top paper off 1 sheet of dough. Cut stars with floured 2-in. cutter. Place 1 in. apart on baking sheets.

5 Bake 8 to 10 minutes until lightly golden at edges. Cool slightly on sheet on a wire rack, then transfer to rack to cool completely. Press scraps together and refrigerate.

6 Repeat with another sheet of dough. Transfer to baking sheet; with floured 1-in. star cutter, cut out centers. Carefully remove centers; add to scraps.

7 Bake and cool cutouts as above.

8 Repeat with remaining dough.

9 **To assemble:** Gently spread a scant teaspoon jam on each whole cookie. Dust cutouts with confectioners' sugar. Place on top of whole cookies.

PER COOKIE: 113 cal, 1 g pro, 13 g car, 0 g fiber, 7 g fat (4 g sat fat), 14 mg chol, 25 mg sod

SHAPED COOKIES

Spritz Cookies

MAKES 7 TO 8 DOZEN · PREP: 25 MIN · BAKE: 10 TO 12 MIN PER BATCH

3½ cups all-purpose flour

1 tsp baking powder

3 sticks (1½ cups) unsalted butter, softened

1 cup granulated sugar

1 egg

2 Tbsp milk

1 tsp vanilla extract

½ tsp almond extract

1 Heat oven to 350°F. In large bowl, combine flour and baking powder. In another large bowl, beat butter and sugar with electric mixer until light and fluffy. Beat in egg, milk, vanilla and almond extracts. Gradually, on low speed, beat in flour mixture until just combined.

2 Fill cookie press with dough and desired disks. Press cookies onto ungreased baking sheets. Bake 10 to 12 minutes or until edges are light golden brown. Cool 2 minutes on baking sheet on a wire rack. Remove to rack to cool completely.

PER COOKIE: 54 cal, 1 g pro, 6 g car, 0 g fiber, 3 g fat (2 g sat fat), 10 mg chol, 29 mg sod

ORANGE SPRITZ COOKIES

Substitute orange juice for milk in basic recipe. Omit almond extract. Add 2 Tbsp grated orange zest and, if desired, ¼ cup finely chopped pecans.

PER COOKIE: 54 cal, 1 g pro, 6 g car, 0 g fiber, 3 g fat (2 g sat fat), 10 mg chol, 28 mg sod

GINGERBREAD SPRITZ COOKIES

Substitute firmly packed dark brown sugar for granulated sugar in basic recipe and omit extracts. Add ½ tsp each ground allspice, ground cloves, ground cinnamon and ground ginger.

PER COOKIE: 55 cal, 1 g pro, 6 g car, 0 g fiber, 3 g fat (2 g sat fat), 10 mg chol, 29 mg sod

POTATO CHIP SPRITZ COOKIES

Reduce flour in basic recipe to 2⅔ cups; combine with 1½ cups finely crushed potato chips and baking powder. Reduce granulated sugar to ¾ cup. Omit almond extract.

PER COOKIE: 51 cal, 1 g pro, 5 g car, 0 g fiber, 3 g fat (2 g sat fat), 10 mg chol, 31 mg sod

CREAM CHEESE SPRITZ COOKIES

Substitute 6 oz (¾ of an 8-oz package) cream cheese, softened, for 1 stick (½ cup) butter in basic recipe. Increase granulated sugar to 1¼ cups. Omit almond extract. Add 2 tsp lemon zest.

PER COOKIE: 54 cal, 1 g pro, 7 g car, 0 g fiber, 3 g fat (2 g sat fat), 10 mg chol, 27 mg sod

Lemon Butter Cookies

MAKES 32 · PREP & CHILL: ABOUT 3 HR · BAKE: 10 TO 13 MIN PER BATCH

2 sticks (1 cup) unsalted butter, softened

¾ cup granulated sugar

2 Tbsp freshly grated lemon zest

½ tsp salt

1 large egg plus yolks of 2 large eggs (save whites for another use)

2½ cups all-purpose flour

Egg wash: yolk of 1 large egg beaten with 2 tsp cold water

Decoration: coarse (crystal) sugar or granulated sugar

Storage tip: Store airtight at cool room temperature up to 1 week, or freeze up to 1 month.

Tip: If dough breaks when rolling it out, let it warm briefly at room temperature.

---

1 Beat butter, sugar, lemon zest and salt in a large bowl with mixer on high speed until pale and fluffy. Beat in whole egg and yolks until well blended. Reduce speed to low, add flour and beat just to mix. Divide dough in quarters; shape each into a disk. Wrap each airtight; refrigerate at least 2 hours or until firm.

2 Heat oven to 350°F. Have ready baking sheet(s), a 4½ x 2-in. dove cookie cutter and a ¾-in. heart cookie cutter.

3 On lightly floured wax paper, with a lightly floured rolling pin, roll out 1 disk (keep rest refrigerated) to ¼ in. thick (see Tip). Dipping cookie cutters in flour between cuts, cut out doves, then a heart in center of each. Slide a baking sheet under the wax paper; freeze 5 to 7 minutes until dough is firm. Peel off doves; push out hearts and place doves 2 in. apart on ungreased baking sheet(s). Reroll hearts and scraps. Brush doves with egg wash; sprinkle lightly with coarse sugar. Repeat with remaining disks.

4 Bake 10 to 13 minutes or until cookies are lightly tinged golden around edges. Transfer with a broad spatula to a wire rack to cool.

PER COOKIE: 118 cal, 2 g pro, 14 g car, 0 g fiber, 6 g fat (4 g sat fat), 41 mg chol, 40 mg sod

Kris's Kisses

MAKES 75 · PREP: 10 MIN · BAKE: 3 TO 3¼ HR PER BATCH

Whites of 2 large eggs

⅛ tsp cider vinegar

½ tsp each vanilla and almond extracts

½ cup granulated sugar

½ cup semisweet chocolate mini-chips

Decoration: tiny candy decors

1 Position racks to divide oven in thirds. Heat to 200°F. Line 2 baking sheets with foil. Have ready a large pastry bag fitted with a star tip with opening large enough to accommodate the chips, or drop meringue off tip of a spoon directly onto sheets.

2 Beat egg whites, vinegar and extracts in a large bowl with mixer on medium speed until soft peaks form when beaters are lifted.

3 On high speed, gradually beat in sugar until stiff, white and glossy. Fold in chips.

4 Spoon into prepared piping bag. Pipe dots of meringue between foil and baking sheets at corners to hold foil in place.

5 Pipe small mounds ¾ in. apart on baking sheets. Sprinkle with decors.

6 Bake 3 to 3¼ hours until meringue kisses are dry and crisp all the way through. Cool on sheet on a wire rack. Peel off foil.

PER COOKIE: 15 cal, 0 g pro, 3 g car, 0 g fiber, 0 g fat (0 g sat fat), 0 mg chol, 15 mg sod

Storage tip: Store airtight at room temperature up to 2 months.

Hazelnut Snowballs

MAKES 64 · PREP: 20 MIN · BAKE: ABOUT 15 MIN PER BATCH

1 cup hazelnuts

2 sticks (1 cup) cold unsalted butter, cut in small pieces

1¾ cups confectioners' sugar

2 tsp vanilla extract

2 cups all-purpose flour

1 Heat oven to 350°F. Spread hazelnuts on a rimmed baking sheet. Bake 10 to 12 minutes or until fragrant and skins begin to flake. Cool slightly, wrap in a kitchen towel and rub off skins. Cool, then pick out nuts. Leave oven heating.

2 Finely grind nuts in food processor (don't overprocess). Add butter, ¼ cup of the confectioners' sugar and the vanilla. Process, scraping bowl often to blend. Add flour; process until combined.

3 With lightly floured hands, roll dough into 1-in. balls. Place 1 in. apart on ungreased cookie sheet(s).

4 Bake about 15 minutes or until bottoms are light brown. Cool on sheets on a wire rack 15 minutes. Gently (cookies are fragile) roll warm cookies in remaining confectioners' sugar. Cool, then roll in sugar again. Refrigerate tightly covered with wax paper between layers up to 1 week.

PER COOKIE: 66 cal, 1 g pro, 7 g car, 0 g fiber, 4 g fat (2 g sat fat), 8 mg chol, 1 mg sod

Hazelnut Snowballs (center) and Cornmeal Lemon Drops (recipe page 38).

Cornmeal Lemon Drops

MAKES 48 · PREP: 20 MIN · BAKE: 6 TO 8 MIN PER BATCH

2 sticks (1 cup) unsalted butter, softened

½ cup each granulated sugar and packed light-brown sugar

½ tsp baking soda

¼ tsp salt

2 large eggs

2 tsp freshly grated lemon zest

1 Tbsp lemon juice

1¾ cup all-purpose flour

¾ cup yellow cornmeal

ICING

1½ cups confectioners' sugar

2 Tbsp milk

40 lemon drop candies, finely crushed

> **Storage tip:** Store airtight with wax paper between layers at room temperature up to 1 week.

1 Beat butter, sugars, baking soda and salt in a large bowl with mixer on medium speed until fluffy. Beat in eggs, lemon zest and juice until well blended.

2 On low speed, gradually beat in flour and cornmeal until blended.

3 Heat oven to 350°F. Drop rounded measuring teaspoons of dough 2 in. apart on ungreased baking sheet(s).

4 Bake 6 to 8 minutes or until golden brown around edges. Cool on sheet 1 minute before removing to wire rack to cool completely.

5 Icing: Whisk confectioner's sugar and milk in a bowl until smooth.

6 Scrape icing into a sturdy ziptop bag. Snip tiny tip off 1 corner and pipe a spiral on each cookie. Before icing dries, spoon crushed candies into sieve wire and dust tops. Let dry completely.

PER COOKIE: 104 cal, 1 g pro, 16 g car, 0 g fiber, 4 g fat (2 g sat fat), 19 mg chol, 57 mg sod

Almond-Orange Macaroons

MAKES 38 · PREP: 10 MIN · BAKE: 15 TO 18 MIN PER BATCH

1 can (8 oz) or 1 roll (7 oz) almond paste, cut in small pieces

2/3 cup granulated sugar

Whites from 2 large eggs

1 Tbsp freshly grated orange zest

3/4 cup slivered almonds

Storage tip: Store airtight with wax paper between layers at cool room temperature up to 1 week, or freeze up to 3 months.

1 Heat oven to 325°F. Line baking sheet(s) with foil.

2 Beat almond paste, sugar, egg whites and zest in a medium bowl with mixer on medium speed until smooth. Drop rounded teaspoons 1 in. apart on prepared baking sheet. Sprinkle with almonds to cover; press nuts gently to adhere.

3 Bake 15 to 18 minutes until tops feel firm and dry when lightly pressed. Cool completely on baking sheet on a wire rack. Peel off foil.

PER MACAROON: 54 cal, 1 g pro, 7 g car, 1 g fiber, 3 g fat (0 g sat fat), 0 mg chol, 3 mg sod

Top: Almond-Orange Macaroons; center: Cranberry Double-Chip Cookie (recipe page 40); bottom: Ginger Drops (recipe page 41).

Cranberry Double-Chip Cookies

MAKES 60 · PREP: 15 MIN · BAKE: 8 TO 10 MIN PER BATCH

2 sticks (1 cup) unsalted butter, softened

1 cup packed light-brown sugar

½ cup granulated sugar

2 tsp vanilla extract

2 large eggs

1 tsp baking soda

½ tsp salt

2¼ cups all-purpose flour

4 bars (3½ oz each) bittersweet chocolate, chopped in ½-in. chunks

2 bars (3½ oz each) white chocolate, chopped in ½-in. chunks

2 cups sweetened dried cranberries, ½ cup chopped

1 Heat oven to 375°F. Have baking sheet(s) ready.

2 Beat butter, sugars and vanilla in a large bowl with mixer on medium speed until fluffy. Beat in eggs, baking soda and salt until blended (mixture will look curdled). On low speed, beat in flour just until blended. Stir in all the chocolate and 1½ cups unchopped cranberries. Drop heaping tablespoons 2 in. apart on ungreased baking sheet. Sprinkle with chopped cranberries.

3 Bake 8 to 10 minutes until edges are golden brown. Cool on sheet on a wire rack about 2 minutes before removing to rack to cool completely.

PER COOKIE: 131 cal, 1 g pro, 18 g car, 1 g fiber, 7 g fat (4 g sat fat), 16 mg chol, 48 mg sod

> *Storage tip:* Store airtight at cool room temperature with wax paper between layers up to 1 week, or freeze up to 3 months.

Ginger Drops

2 sticks (1 cup) unsalted butter, softened

½ cup each packed dark-brown sugar and granulated sugar

4 tsp ground ginger

1 tsp each baking powder and baking soda

1 tsp finely ground pepper

1 tsp vanilla extract

1 large egg

⅓ cup robust (unsulphured) molasses

2½ cups all-purpose flour

⅓ cup minced crystallized ginger

ICING

1½ cups confectioners' sugar

½ tsp ground ginger

2 Tbsp milk

Decoration: red and green nonpareils

1 Heat oven to 350°F. Line baking sheet(s) with foil.

2 Beat butter, sugars, ginger, baking powder, baking soda, pepper and vanilla in a large bowl with mixer on high speed until pale and fluffy.

3 Add egg; beat until blended. Beat in molasses. On low speed, beat in flour and minced ginger. Drop heaping teaspoons 1 in. apart on prepared baking sheet.

4 Bake 8 to 10 minutes until light brown on top. Cool on sheet 2 minutes before removing to a wire rack to cool completely.

5 Icing: Stir ingredients in a small bowl until smooth. Using a fork, drizzle over cookies, then sprinkle with nonpareils. Let icing dry at least 30 minutes.

PER COOKIE: 85 cal, 1 g pro, 13 g car, 0 g fiber, 3 g fat (2 g sat fat), 12 mg chol, 47 mg sod

---

Storage tip: Store airtight at cool room temperature with wax paper between layers up to 1 week, or freeze up to 3 months.

Delightfully peppery, these will probably appeal more to adults

Pine Nut Macaroons

MAKES 24 · PREP: 15 MIN · BAKE: 22 TO 25 MIN PER BATCH

1 can (8 oz) or 1 roll (7 oz) almond paste (no substitutions), cut in small pieces

2/3 cup granulated sugar

Whites from 2 large eggs

1 tsp freshly grated lemon zest

3/4 cup pine nuts (see Note)

1 Heat oven to 325°F. Line baking sheet(s) with foil.

2 Beat first 4 ingredients in a medium bowl with mixer on medium speed until smooth. Drop heaping teaspoonfuls 1 in. apart on prepared baking sheet(s). Sprinkle with pine nuts to cover; press nuts gently to adhere.

3 Bake 22 to 25 minutes until tops feel firm and dry when lightly pressed. Cool completely on baking sheet on a wire rack. Peel off foil.

PER MACAROON: 95 cal, 2 g pro, 11 g car, 1 g fiber, 6 g fat (0 g sat fat), 0 mg chol, 6 mg sod

> **Storage tip:** These are best eaten within 2 weeks, or they can be frozen up to 3 months.

Note: Pine nuts packed in bags are less expensive than those in small jars. Look for them in health food and warehouse stores and in the bulk-food section of your supermarket.

Chocolate-Dipped Macaroons

MAKES 48 · PREP: 30 MIN · BAKE: 14 TO 16 MIN PER BATCH

1 can (14 oz) sweetened condensed milk (not evaporated milk)

1 bag (14 oz) sweetened flaked coconut

1 Tbsp freshly grated orange zest

1 tsp vanilla extract

Whites from 2 large eggs

1 bag (12 oz) semisweet chocolate chips

PER MACAROON: 99 cal, 1 g pro, 13 g car, 1 g fiber, 5 g fat (4 g sat fat), 3 mg chol, 37 mg sod

1 Heat oven to 325°F. Line baking sheet(s) with foil. Coat with cooking spray and dust with flour.

2 Mix condensed milk, coconut, orange zest and vanilla in a large bowl. Beat egg whites in a small to medium bowl with mixer on high speed until stiff peaks form when beaters are lifted. Fold into coconut mixture. Drop level measuring tablespoons about 1 in. apart on baking sheet(s).

3 Bake 14 to 16 minutes until lightly toasted. Slide foil onto a wire rack. Let cool completely. Peel off foil; save foil.

4 Melt chocolate chips as package directs. Dip bottoms of macaroons in chocolate. Replace on foil. Slide foil back onto baking sheets. Refrigerate until chocolate sets; peel macaroons off foil. Refrigerate tightly covered, with wax paper between layers, up to 1 week.

DROP COOKIES

Italian Anise Cookies

MAKES 80 · PREP: 25 MIN · BAKE: 8 TO 10 MIN

¾ cup granulated sugar

1 stick (½ cup) unsalted butter, melted

2 large eggs

¼ cup milk

1 tsp anise extract

2¾ cups all-purpose flour

2½ tsp baking powder

¼ tsp salt

GLAZE

1 cup confectioners' sugar

4 to 5 tsp milk

1 tsp anise extract

Decoration: multicolored nonpareils

> **Storage tip:** Store airtight at room temperature up to 2 weeks, or freeze up to 1 month.

1 Heat oven to 325°F. Coat baking sheet(s) with cooking spray.

2 Dough: Beat sugar, melted butter, eggs, milk and anise extract in a large bowl with mixer until blended. On low speed, beat in flour, baking powder and salt until blended.

3 Drop rounded measuring teaspoons of dough 2 in. apart onto the prepared baking sheet(s).

4 Bake 8 to 10 minutes or until bottoms are light golden. Remove cookies to a wire rack to cool.

5 Glaze: Whisk confectioners' sugar, milk and anise extract in a small bowl until smooth.

6 Dip tops of cookies in Glaze and, while wet, sprinkle with nonpareils. Let set.

PER COOKIE: 45 cal, 1 g pro, 8 g car, 0 g fiber, 1 g fat (1 g sat fat), 8 mg chol, 40 mg sod

Oatmeal Cookies

MAKES 35 · PREP: 25 MIN · BAKE: 15 TO 16 MIN PER BATCH

1 cup (2 sticks) unsalted butter, softened

1 cup packed brown sugar

½ cup granulated sugar

2 eggs

1 tsp vanilla extract

2 cups all-purpose flour

1 tsp baking powder

½ tsp baking soda

½ tsp salt

2 cups uncooked old-fashioned oats

1 Heat oven to 350°F. Beat butter and sugars in large bowl with electric mixer at medium speed until light and fluffy. Beat in eggs, one at a time, beating well after each. Add vanilla; mix well. In a separate bowl, combine flour, baking powder, baking soda, salt and oats. Add to batter mixture all at once; blend well.

2 Scoop tablespoonfulls of dough onto baking sheets, leaving 1 in. between cookies. Press cookies down slightly.

3 Bake 15 to 16 minutes or until golden brown. Cool on sheets 5 minutes; transfer to a wire rack to cool completely.

PER COOKIE: 129 cal, 2 g pro, 18 g car, 1 g fiber, 6 g fat (3 g sat fat), 26 mg chol, 108 mg sod

BANANA WALNUT: Replace vanilla extract with banana extract and add 1 tsp ground cinnamon to flour mixture. Stir in ⅔ cup finely chopped dried banana chips and 1 cup chopped walnuts after flour mixture.
PER COOKIE: 157 cal, 2 g pro, 19 g car, 1 g fiber, 8 g fat (4 g sat fat), 26 mg chol, 110 mg sod

KEY LIME: Beat in 3 Tbsp freshly grated lime zest (3 medium limes) to butter and sugar mixture. **PER COOKIE:** 129 cal, 2 g pro, 18 g car, 1 g fiber, 6 g fat (3 g sat fat), 26 mg chol, 108 mg sod

CHOCOLATE MALTED: Add ½ cup malted milk powder to flour mixture. Stir in 1 cup chopped malted milk balls after flour mixture.
PER COOKIE: 157 cal, 2 g pro, 22 g car, 1 g fiber, 7 g fat (4 g sat fat), 27 mg chol, 133 mg sod

CRANBERRY-ORANGE: Beat in 2 Tbsp freshly grated orange zest (2 large oranges) to butter and sugar mixture. Stir in 1 cup dried cranberries after flour mixture.
PER COOKIE: 140 cal, 2 g pro, 21 g car, 1 g fiber, 6 g fat (3 g sat fat), 26 mg chol, 110 mg sod

COFFEE TOFFEE: Beat in 1 Tbsp instant coffee to butter and sugar mixture. Stir in 1 package (8 oz) or 1½ cups English toffee bits after flour mixture.
PER COOKIE: 164 cal, 2 g pro, 22 g car, 1 g fiber, 8 g fat (4 g sat fat), 28 mg chol, 136 mg sod

BARS

Double Mint Squares

MAKES 36 · PREP: 25 MIN · BAKE: 30 TO 35 MIN

¾ cup mint chocolate chips

BATTER

1½ sticks (¾ cup) unsalted butter

1 cup granulated sugar

3 large eggs

½ tsp each vanilla and mint extract

1⅓ cups all-purpose flour

1 tsp baking powder

8 drops green liquid food color

GLAZE

¾ cup mint chocolate chips

2 Tbsp stick unsalted butter

1 Tbsp light corn syrup

Decoration: ¼ cup crushed red-and-white striped candy canes (about 2) or crushed red-and-white mint candies

Planning tip: Refrigerate airtight with wax paper between layers up to 1 week.

1 Heat oven to 350°F. Line a 9-in.-square baking pan with foil, letting ends extend above pan 2 in. on opposite sides. Coat foil with cooking spray.

2 Melt ¾ cup mint chocolate chips as package directs. Cool slightly.

3 Batter: Melt butter in a medium saucepan. Remove from heat; whisk in sugar. Stir in eggs and extracts, then flour and baking powder until just blended.

4 Add 1¼ cups Batter to the melted chocolate; stir until blended. Spread evenly in prepared pan.

5 Stir green food color into remaining batter until evenly tinted. Carefully pour over chocolate batter, then gently spread into an even layer.

6 Bake 30 to 35 minutes or until lightly brown on top and a wooden pick inserted in center comes out with moist crumbs attached. Cool in pan on a wire rack.

7 Glaze: Melt chips and butter in a small saucepan over low heat or in a bowl in microwave. Stir in corn syrup until blended. Cool 5 minutes or until no longer hot, but still spreadable. Spread over brownie; sprinkle with crushed candy. Chill until firm.

8 Lift foil by ends onto cutting board. Cut into 36 squares.

PER SQUARE: 114 cal, 1 g pro, 14 g car, 0 g fiber, 6 g fat (3 g sat fat), 30 mg chol, 66 mg sod

Apricot Linzer Bars

MAKES 64 · PREP: 10 MIN · BAKE: ABOUT 25 MIN

2 sticks (1 cup) unsalted butter or margarine (not spread), softened

1 cup confectioners' sugar

1 Tbsp cinnamon

2 tsp vanilla extract

1 cup all-purpose flour

½ cup each whole hazelnuts and sliced natural (with skin) almonds, coarsely ground (see Tip)

1 cup (12 oz) apricot preserves

Decoration: melted white chocolate

Planning tip: Store airtight at room temperature with waxed paper between layers up to 1 week.

Tip: Grind the nuts in a food processor, but don't overprocess or you'll wind up with a thick paste.

---

1 Heat oven to 350°F. Line a 13 x 9-in. baking pan with foil, letting foil extend about 2 in. above opposite ends.

2 Beat butter, sugar, cinnamon and vanilla in a large bowl with mixer on high speed until fluffy. On low speed, beat in flour and nuts. Spread in pan.

3 Bake 25 minutes or until set and browned. Cool in pan on a wire rack just until warm. Spread with preserves; cool completely.

4 Holding foil by ends, lift to cutting board. Make 7 evenly spaced cuts lengthwise (to make 8 strips), then 7 evenly spaced cuts crosswise. Drizzle with melted white chocolate.

PER BAR: 63 cal, 1 g pro, 7 g car, 0 g fiber, 4 g fat (2 g sat fat), 8 mg chol, 32 mg sod

---

RASPBERRY LINZER DIAMONDS

Prepare as directed in recipe, substituting raspberry jam for apricot preserves. Make 7 cuts lengthwise (to make 8 strips), then cut diagonally crosswise to make 9 diamonds per strip with a triangle at each end. Decorate with sliced almonds.

MAKES 72 DIAMONDS, 16 TRIANGLES.

Raspberry Schnitten

MAKES 32 · PREP AND CHILL: ABOUT 1 HR 20 MIN · BAKE: 15 TO 20 MIN

1 stick (½ cup) unsalted butter, softened

⅓ cup granulated sugar

1 large egg

2 cups all-purpose flour

½ cup seedless raspberry jam

⅓ cup hazelnuts, toasted and chopped (see Note)

Decoration: 1 cup semisweet chocolate chips (see Tip)

Storage tip: Store airtight at cool room temperature with wax paper between layers up to 1 week, or freeze up to 1 month.

Tip: If you wish, substitute white chocolate chips for half or all of the chocolate chips.

1 Beat butter and sugar in medium bowl with mixer on high speed until fluffy. Beat in egg, reduce speed to low and gradually add flour until blended. Divide dough in half; wrap in plastic wrap. Chill 1 hour or until firm enough to roll out.

2 Heat oven to 350°F. Have a baking sheet ready.

3 Place each portion of dough between 2 sheets of wax paper; roll each into a 15 x 4-in. rectangle. Peel paper off top of both rectangles; invert dough 2 in. apart on ungreased baking sheet. Peel off wax paper.

4 Fold long sides of dough inward ½ in., keeping borders even. Pat edges to keep sides straight and seal any cracks. Carefully spread half the jam on each rectangle up to turned-in edges. Sprinkle jam with nuts.

5 Bake 15 to 20 minutes until edges are light golden. Cool on pan on a wire rack 5 minutes. While still warm, cut each rectangle in 16 slices. Remove to rack to cool completely.

6 **To decorate:** Melt chocolate in a small bowl in microwave as package directs. Dip ends of cookies in melted chocolate, scraping excess off bottom against edge of bowl. Place on wax paper. Refrigerate or leave in a cool place until chocolate sets.

PER BAR: 111 cal, 1 g pro, 15 g car, 1 g fiber, 6 g fat (3 g sat fat), 14 mg chol, 23 mg sod

Note: To toast hazelnuts, spread nuts on a rimmed baking sheet or pie plate. Bake in a 325°F oven 15 to 18 minutes, stirring occasionally, until skins begin to brown lightly and flake. Turn out onto a clean kitchen towel. Rub off most of skins. Cool, then chop.

Pecan-Date Squares

MAKES 40 · PREP: 25 MIN · BAKE: 35 MIN

FILLING

1 lb (3 cups) pitted dates, chopped

1½ cups orange juice

CRUST & TOPPING

1½ cups all-purpose flour

1½ cups old-fashioned oats

⅔ cup packed light-brown sugar

1½ cups pecans, chopped

2½ sticks (1¼ cups) cold unsalted butter, cut up

Decoration: confectioners' sugar

Storage tip: Refrigerate tightly covered with wax paper between layers up to 2 weeks, or freeze up to 1 month.

---

1 Filling: Bring dates and orange juice to a boil in a 3-qt saucepan. Reduce heat to low and simmer, stirring often, 15 minutes or until dates are tender, orange juice is absorbed and mixture thickens. Set aside to cool.

2 Heat oven to 350°F. Line a 13 x 9-in. baking pan with foil, letting foil extend 2 in. above pan at opposite ends. Lightly coat with cooking spray.

3 Crust & Topping: Put flour, oats, brown sugar and ½ cup of the chopped pecans in food processor; pulse to blend. Add butter; pulse until mixture is crumbly. Transfer 2½ cups crumb mixture to a medium bowl. Press remaining crumbs over bottom of lined pan. Spoon filling over crust and carefully spread in an even layer, up to ¼ in. from edge. Stir remaining pecans into bowl with crumb mixture, sprinkle over filling and press down lightly with fingertips.

4 Bake 35 minutes or until edges are brown. Cool completely in baking pan on a wire rack.

5 Lift foil by ends to cutting board. Cut into 1½-in. squares. Dust with confectioners' sugar.

PER BAR: 161 cal, 2 g pro, 20 g car, 2 g fiber, 9 g fat (4 g sat fat), 15 mg chol, 42 mg sod

Pecan-Date Squares and Raspberry Cheesecake Bars (see recipe page 56).

Raspberry Cheesecake Bars

MAKES 36 · PREP & CHILL: 4 HR 25 MIN · BAKE: 45 TO 53 MIN

CRUST

18 shortbread cookies (from a 10-oz box)

3 Tbsp unsalted butter, softened

1 jar (12 oz) seedless red raspberry jam

FILLING

2 bricks (8 oz each) ⅓-less-fat cream cheese (Neufchâtel), at room temperature

1⅓ cups granulated sugar

3 large eggs, at room temperature

2 Tbsp freshly grated lemon zest

1 Heat oven to 300°F. Line a 13 x 9-in. baking pan with foil, letting foil extend about 2 in. above opposite ends of pan. Lightly coat with cooking spray.

2 **Crust:** Pulse cookies in food processor to fine crumbs. Add butter; pulse until blended. Remove processor blade; scrape crumb mixture into lined pan; press evenly over bottom. Bake 10 to 13 minutes or until lightly browned. Cool on a wire rack 10 minutes.

3 Remove and reserve 2 Tbsp jam. Spread remaining jam over crust up to ¾ in. from edge.

4 **Filling:** Beat cream cheese and sugar in a large bowl with mixer on high speed until smooth. On medium speed, beat in eggs and lemon zest just to blend. Spoon around edges over jam, then pour over jam in middle. Heat remaining 2 Tbsp jam, stirring until runny. Spoon into a small ziptop bag, cut a tip off one corner and drizzle on filling.

5 Bake 35 to 40 minutes until set around edges but jiggly in center. Cool in pan on a wire rack. Refrigerate at least 4 hours or overnight before cutting.

6 Lift foil by ends onto a cutting board. Cut into 36 bars.

PER BAR: 117 cal, 2 g pro, 16 g car, 0 g fiber, 5 g fat (3 g sat fat), 30 mg chol, 79 mg sod

Classic Brownies

MAKES 16 · PREP: 20 MIN · BAKE: 30 TO 33 MIN

5 Tbsp cold unsalted butter, cut in pieces

4 oz bittersweet chocolate, coarsely chopped

2 oz unsweetened baking chocolate, coarsely chopped

¾ cup granulated sugar

2 large eggs

1 tsp vanilla extract

½ tsp instant espresso powder (optional, but really good)

¼ tsp salt

⅓ cup all-purpose flour

1 cup chopped walnuts

1 Heat oven to 325°F. Line an 8-in. square baking pan with foil; butter the foil.

2 Microwave the butter and chocolates in a medium bowl, stirring every 10 seconds, until melted and blended. Cool slightly; then, with a whisk, stir in sugar (mixture will become grainy). Whisk in eggs, 1 at a time. Whisk in vanilla. Gently stir in espresso powder, salt and flour just until blended. With a rubber spatula, fold in walnuts. Scrape batter into prepared pan; smooth top.

3 Bake 30 to 33 minutes until top is dull and a wooden pick inserted in center comes out with moist, chocolate-streaked crumbs attached. Cool in pan on a wire rack.

4 Invert on rack, peel off foil and invert onto a cutting board. Cut into 16 squares.

PER BROWNIE: 191 cal, 3 g pro, 18 g car, 1 g fiber, 13 g fat (5 g sat fat), 37 mg chol, 46 mg sod

> **Planning tip:** Best served within 2 days, wrapped in plastic wrap and left at room temperature. Or wrap airtight and freeze up to 2 months.

White Chocolate Strawberry Squares

MAKES 36 · PREP: ABOUT 15 MIN · BAKE: 50 TO 55 MIN

1 stick (½ cup) unsalted butter

1¾ cups white chocolate chips (morsels)

2 large eggs

½ cup granulated sugar

1 tsp almond extract

1½ cups all-purpose flour

1 cup strawberry preserves or jam (see Tip)

⅓ cup sliced natural almonds

1 Heat oven to 350°F. Line a 9-in.-square pan with foil, letting it extend 2 in. above pan on opposite sides. Coat with cooking spray.

2 Melt butter and 1½ cups white chocolate chips in a medium saucepan over low heat (mixture may look curdled).

3 Beat eggs and sugar in a large bowl with mixer on medium-high speed until lemon colored. Stir in white chocolate mixture and extract until combined, then the flour just until blended. Remove and reserve ½ cup batter. Spread remaining batter in prepared pan.

4 Bake 20 minutes or until light golden. Gently spread preserves evenly over crust. Spoon dollops of reserved batter over top; sprinkle with almonds.

5 Bake 30 to 35 minutes until lightly browned. Cool in pan on a wire rack.

6 Lift by foil ends to a cutting board. Melt remaining ¼ cup white chocolate chips as pkg directs. Scrape into a small, sturdy plastic ziptop bag. Snip off tip of a corner and drizzle top with back-and-forth lines. Let set. Cut in 36 squares; remove from foil.

PER BAR: 130 cal, 2 g pro, 17 g car, 0 g fiber, 6 g fat (3 g sat fat), 20 mg chol, 31 mg sod

Storage tip: Refrigerate airtight up to 1 week, or freeze up to 1 month.

Tip: Raspberry preserves or jam can be substituted.

Chocolate Chip Bars

MAKES 2 TO 3 DOZEN · PREP: 20 MIN · BAKE: 25 TO 30 MIN

Heat oven to 350°F. Coat 9 x 13 in. baking pan with cooking spray. Using 2 packages (18 oz each) refrigerated chocolate chip cookie dough, choose one of the following variations:

CRANBERRY CHOCOLATE In large bowl, knead together cookie dough, 1 cup dried cranberries and ½ cup chopped pecans. Press dough into prepared pan. Bake 25 to 30 minutes or until edges are light golden brown. Cool completely in pan on wire rack. Drizzle with ⅓ cup semisweet chocolate chips, melted. Cut into bars or other shapes.

PER BAR: 190 cal, 2 g pro, 27 g car, 1 g fiber, 9 g fat (3 g sat fat), 0 mg chol, 107 mg sod

CRISPY CHOCOLATE PEANUT BUTTER In large bowl, knead together cookie dough, 6 oz (about 1 cup) of milk chocolate chips, 6 oz (about ½ cup) peanut butter chips, 1 cup chopped pretzels and 1 cup crisp rice cereal. Press dough into prepared pan. Bake 25 to 30 minutes or until edges are light golden brown. Remove pan from oven and immediately sprinkle with remaining chocolate and peanut butter chips from package; if desired, swirl in zigzag motion. Cool completely in pan on wire rack. Cut into rectangles.

PER BAR: 286 cal, 5 g pro, 36 g car, 1 g fiber, 13 g fat (7 g sat fat), 3 mg chol, 186 mg sod

WHITE CHOCOLATE APRICOT In large bowl, knead together cookie dough, 6 oz (about 1 cup) white chocolate chips and a full package (7 oz) chopped dried apricots. Press dough into prepared pan; sprinkle with 1 cup chopped pecans. Bake 25 to 30 minutes or until edges are light golden brown. Cool completely in pan on wire rack. Melt ⅓ cup white chocolate chips; drizzle over cooled bars. Cut in squares or bars.

PER BAR: 241 cal, 3 g pro, 31 g car, 2 g fiber, 12 g fat (4 g sat fat), 2 mg chol, 115 mg sod

CARAMEL APPLE In large bowl, combine 4 Granny Smith apples, peeled, cored and chopped, ½ cup firmly packed brown sugar, 1 Tbsp lemon juice. Press dough into prepared pan. Top with apple mixture. Drizzle with ½ cup caramel ice cream topping combined with 1 tsp all-purpose flour. Bake 25 to 30 minutes or until edges are golden brown. Cool completely in pan on wire rack.

PER BAR: 191 cal, 2 g pro, 31 g car, 1 g fiber, 7 g fat (2 g sat fat), 0 mg chol, 127 mg sod

COCONUT MACADAMIA: In large bowl, combine 2 cups sweetened flaked coconut, 1 cup chopped macadamia nuts, ½ cup packed brown sugar and 1 tsp rum extract. Press dough into prepared pan; top with coconut mixture. Bake 25 to 30 minutes or until edges are golden brown. Cool completely in pan on cooling rack. Cut into rounds or other shapes.

PER BAR: 224 cal, 2 g pro, 28 g car, 1 g fiber, 12 g fat (4 g sat fat), 0 mg chol, 120 mg sod

Brown Sugar-Pecan Sticky Bars

MAKES 36 · PREP: ABOUT 15 MIN · BAKE: 20 TO 30 MIN

1 cup old-fashioned oats

1¼ cups packed light-brown sugar

1½ sticks (¾ cup) unsalted butter, slightly softened

⅛ tsp salt

1 large egg

1¼ tsp vanilla extract

1⅓ cups all-purpose flour

1 cup chopped pecans

¾ cup sweetened flaked coconut

TOPPING

¾ cup (about 3 oz) chopped pecans

½ stick (¼ cup) unsalted butter, cut up

⅔ cup packed light-brown sugar

Pinch of salt

¼ cup heavy (whipping) cream

2½ Tbsp light corn syrup

1 tsp vanilla extract

1 Position racks to divide oven in thirds. Heat to 350°F. Line a 13 x 9-in. baking pan with foil, letting foil extend 2 in. above pan at opposite ends. Coat with cooking spray.

2 Mix oats and ¼ cup hot water in a small bowl. In a large bowl with mixer, beat brown sugar, butter and salt 2 minutes or until fluffy. Beat in egg and vanilla. On low speed, beat in flour and oat mixture until blended. Fold in nuts and coconut. Spread in prepared pan.

3 Bake in upper third of oven 25 to 30 minutes until top is browned and a pick inserted in center comes out clean. Place pan on a wire rack (crust should be warm when topping is added).

4 Topping: Bring pecans and butter to a simmer in a heavy 2-qt saucepan over medium-high heat. Cook, stirring, 2 to 4 minutes or until butter is browned (take care it doesn't burn). Using a long-handled wooden spoon to avoid spattering, stir in brown sugar, salt, cream and corn syrup. Return to a boil and, stirring, boil briskly exactly 2 minutes (mixture will resemble caramel sauce). Remove from heat; stir in vanilla. Spread over warm crust. Let cool.

5 Cut in bars with a large knife dipped in hot water and dried between cuts.

PER BAR: 176 cal, 2 g pro, 20 g car, 1 g fiber, 11 g fat (4 g sat fat), 22 mg chol, 24 mg sod

Storage tip: Store airtight at room temperature up to 1 week, or freeze up to 1 month.

Yule Log

SERVES 10 · PREP & CHILL: 2½ HR

FILLING & FROSTING

2 cups heavy (whipping) cream

¾ cup bottled caramel ice cream topping

1 box (9 oz) chocolate wafer cookies (Nabisco Famous Chocolate Wafers)

Tree stumps: *2 chocolate-covered cream-filled cake rolls (such as Ho Hos or Yodels), diagonally trimmed at ends, then cut in half*

Decoration: *Marshmallow Mushrooms (directions follow) and unsweetened cocoa powder*

> **Planning tip:** May be made through Step 3 up to 1 day ahead.

1 Have ready a serving platter or tray at least 15 in. long and 4 in. wide.

2 Filling & Frosting: Beat cream and caramel topping in a large bowl with mixer on high speed until stiff peaks form when beaters are lifted.

3 Spread scant 1 Tbsp Filling & Frosting on each wafer. Begin stacking wafers together, laying stacks in 1 long row on serving platter. Glue stumps onto log with Filling & Frosting. Frost log and stumps to resemble bark, leaving ends of stumps unfrosted. Refrigerate at least 2 hours or up to 1 day.

4 To serve: Dust log and stumps with cocoa. Decorate with Marshmallow Mushrooms. Slice roll at a 45-degree angle.

PER SERVING (without mushrooms): 338 cal, 3 g pro, 37 g car, 1 g fiber, 21 g fat (12 g saturated fat), 68 mg chol, 287 mg sod

MARSHMALLOW MUSHROOMS Flatten 6 regular-size marshmallows. Shape into mushroom caps over top of a finger. Cut 3 marshmallows in half lengthwise. Roll each half into a stem. Moisten 1 end of stem with water and press into cap. Dip cap into cocoa powder; brush off excess.

Neapolitan Ice Cream Cake

SERVES 12 · PREP & FREEZE: 1¼ HR

1 cup heavy (whipping) cream or 2 cups nondairy whipped topping

¼ cup confectioners' sugar

½-gal block Neapolitan ice cream

About 12 imported Italian savoiardi ladyfingers (see Note), or other crisp 3½- to 4-in.-long cookies

2 Tbsp bottled chocolate syrup

¼ cup each chopped hazelnuts or almonds and fresh strawberries

Tip: If desired, a star piping tip can be inserted into the cutoff corner of the ziptop bag before piping the cream around the top.

Planning tip: May be made through Step 4 up to 1 week ahead.

1 Using plastic wrap, line a plate or cutting board large enough to freeze cake on.

2 Beat cream and sugar in a medium bowl with mixer on high speed until stiff peaks form when beaters are lifted.

3 Open top of ice cream carton, then sides and ends. Lift block of ice cream with a spatula onto lined plate. Spread sides with about ¾ cup whipped cream. Press cookies upright into cream.

4 Scrape remaining cream into a large, sturdy ziptop bag (see Tip). Cut tip off 1 corner and pipe cream on ice cream along both rows of cookies. Freeze at least 1 hour or, when hard, remove from plate, wrap airtight with plastic wrap and freeze up to 1 week.

5 To serve: Unwrap, place on serving platter and drizzle top with chocolate syrup. Scatter nuts and berries down middle. Using a long serrated knife, slice crosswise between cookies. Cut slices in half.

PER SERVING: 321 cal, 5 g pro, 38 g car, 1 g fiber, 18 g fat (9 g saturated fat), 62 mg chol, 95 mg sod

Note: Imported Italian savoiardi ladyfingers are crisp and longer than the familiar sponge cake-like variety.

Almond Macaroon Ice Cream Cake

SERVES 12 · PREP & FREEZE: 5½ HR

2 pt chocolate ice cream

1 pkg (13 oz) soft coconut macaroons (such as Archway)

2 pt vanilla Swiss almond ice cream (we used Häagen-Dazs)

½ cup (from a 7.25-oz bottle) chocolate shell ice cream topping

1 cup sliced almonds, toasted (see Note)

1 Remove chocolate ice cream from freezer; let stand 15 minutes until slightly softened.

2 Meanwhile lightly coat an 8 x 3-in. springform pan with cooking spray. Pull apart half the macaroons to make coarse crumbs. Press lightly over bottom and ½ in. up sides of pan. Spread chocolate ice cream evenly over crust.

3 Break remaining macaroons into coarse crumbs. Sprinkle evenly over chocolate ice cream. Freeze 45 minutes or until almost firm.

4 Soften vanilla Swiss almond ice cream as above. Spread evenly over top of cake and freeze at least 4 hours or until firm.

5 Pour chocolate topping on middle of cake; tilt pan to cover top completely. Let topping harden 5 minutes.

6 Wrap pan with a warm, damp kitchen towel 1 minute to loosen sides. Remove pan sides; pat almonds onto sides of cake. (If ice cream is too hard for almonds to stick, leave cake at room temperature 5 to 10 minutes.)

PER SERVING: 464 cal, 5 g pro, 47 g car, 0 g fiber, 30 g fat (15 g sat fat), 45 mg chol, 130 mg sod

---

Planning tip: Can be made up to 1 week ahead. Wrap in plastic wrap, then foil, and freeze.

Note: To toast almonds, spread in a baking pan and bake in a 350°F oven, stirring once or twice to assure even browning, 7 to 10 minutes until fragrant and light golden brown. Let cool.

Holly Cupcake Wreath

MAKES 12 CUPCAKES · PREP: 40 MIN · BAKE: 20 TO 25 MIN

BATTER

¾ stick (6 Tbsp) unsalted butter, softened

½ cup packed light-brown sugar

2 tsp ground ginger

1 tsp ground cinnamon

½ tsp each baking powder and baking soda

¼ tsp each ground cloves and allspice

¼ tsp salt

1 large egg

⅓ cup reduced-fat sour cream

⅓ cup light molasses

1⅓ cups all-purpose flour

FROSTING

1 cup white chocolate chips

1½ sticks (¾ cup) unsalted butter, softened

2 cups confectioners' sugar

¼ cup cold reduced-fat sour cream

1 tsp vanilla extract

Holly Leaf Cookies (directions follow)

Holly berries: 36 red hot cinnamon candies or other small, round, red candies

1 Heat oven to 350°F. Line 12 regular size (2½-in. diameter) muffin cups with paper or foil liners.

2 Batter: Beat butter, sugar, ginger, cinnamon, baking powder, baking soda, cloves, allspice and salt in a large bowl with mixer on medium-high speed until fluffy and lighter in color. On low speed, add egg, sour cream and molasses; beat until well blended (batter will look curdled). Beat in flour until just blended. Spoon evenly into lined cups.

3 Bake 20 to 25 minutes until a wooden pick inserted in centers comes out clean. Cool completely in pan on a wire rack.

4 Frosting: Melt chips as directed on package. Scrape into a large bowl; cool slightly. Add butter and beat with mixer on medium until blended and smooth. Add remaining ingredients; beat on low speed until blended. Increase speed to high; beat about 5 minutes until thick and fluffy (if frosting doesn't thicken, chill 5 minutes and beat again). Pipe or spread on cooled cupcakes. Refrigerate 20 minutes or until frosting is firm.

5 To serve: Press 3 Holly Leaf Cookies and Holly berries on each cupcake.

PER CUPCAKE (without leaf cookies and berries): 461 cal, 3 g pro, 60 g car, 0 g fiber, 25 g fat (16 g saturated fat), 68 mg chol, 168 mg sod

> *Planning tip:* Cupcakes can be frosted up to 3 days ahead. Refrigerate covered. Add cookies and candies no more than 3 hours before serving.

Holly Leaf Cookies

1 stick (1/2 cup) unsalted butter or margarine (not spread), softened

1/2 cup granulated sugar

1/4 tsp salt

1 tsp vanilla extract

1 large egg

1 1/4 cups all-purpose flour

Green crystal sugar

1 Beat butter, sugar, salt and vanilla in a large bowl with mixer on medium speed 3 minutes or until fluffy. Beat in egg. On low speed, beat in flour just until blended. Shape dough into a disk. Wrap airtight; refrigerate 1 1/2 hours or until firm.

2 Heat oven to 375°F. Have ready a 2 x 1-in. holly-leaf cookie cutter and green sanding (crystal) sugar (found in supermarkets or crafts stores).

3 On lightly floured wax paper with a lightly floured rolling pin, roll out 1 disk dough to 1/4 in. thick. Dipping cookie cutter in flour between cuts, cut out 36 holly leaves. Reroll and cut scraps.

4 Dip 1 side of each leaf into green sugar (if dough is too soft, refrigerate until more manageable). Place sugar side up, 1 in. apart on ungreased baking sheet(s). Bake 7 to 9 minutes or until lightly brown around edges. Cool on sheet(s) on a wire rack 5 minutes before removing cookies to rack to cool completely.

Marble Pound Cake

MAKES 1 LOAF, 12 SLICES · PREP: 30 MIN · BAKE: ABOUT 1 HR 20 MIN

3/4 cup semisweet chocolate chips

2 sticks (1 cup) unsalted butter or margarine (not spread), softened

1 1/2 cups granulated sugar

1 1/2 tsp baking powder

1/4 tsp salt

5 large eggs, at room temperature

1 1/2 tsp vanilla extract

2 1/4 cups all-purpose flour

Decoration: 3 Tbsp each semisweet chocolate and white chocolate chips, and 1 tsp vegetable oil

---

Planning tip: Wrapped undecorated cake can be kept at room temperature up to 1 week, or frozen up to 2 months. Decorate at least 1 hour before serving.

---

1 Heat oven to 325°F. Grease a 9 x 5 x 3-in. loaf pan (preferably nonstick); line bottom with wax paper.

2 Melt chocolate chips as package directs; cool to room temperature. In a large bowl with mixer on high speed, beat butter, sugar, baking powder and salt 3 minutes or until pale and fluffy. Beat in eggs, 1 at a time. Beat in vanilla. On low speed, beat in flour just until blended.

3 Spoon 1 1/2 cups batter into a medium bowl; stir in melted chocolate until blended. Drop spoonfuls plain and chocolate batter alternately in prepared pan. Run a knife through batters for a marbelized effect.

4 Bake 1 hour 20 minutes or until a wooden pick inserted in center comes out clean. Cool in pan on a wire rack 15 minutes, invert on rack, remove wax paper, turn cake right side up and cool completely.

5 To decorate: Place cake on wax paper. Separately melt semisweet and white chocolate chips as packages direct; stir 1/2 tsp oil into each until blended. Spoon each into a sturdy ziptop bag, snip tip off a corner and drizzle lines on cake. Let stand until chocolate sets.

PER SLICE: 433 cal, 6 g pro, 53 g car, 1 g fiber, 23 g fat (13 g saturated fat), 130 mg chol, 298 mg sod

Stand-Up Gingerbread House

SERVES 16 · PREP & CHILL: 3¾ HR
BAKE: 10 TO 12 MIN PER BATCH · DECORATE: DEPENDS ON SKILL

COOKIES

½ cup each solid vegetable shortening and unsalted butter (1 stick), melted and cooled

1 cup light molasses

1 cup packed brown sugar

½ cup water

1 large egg

1½ Tbsp ground ginger

1 Tbsp baking soda

1 tsp each ground cloves, cinnamon and nutmeg

1 tsp vanilla extract

6 cups all-purpose flour

Icing & Decorations
(recipe follows)

Planning tip: The dough can be refrigerated up to 1 week, or frozen up to 3 months. The undecorated baked cookies can be stored airtight at cool room temperature up to 2 weeks. Decorated cookies can be stored at room temperature up to 1 week if eating, longer if used just as a decoration.

---

1 Trace outline of house and supporting triangle (printed on page 96) on tracing paper. Cut out, then trace onto heavy cardboard and cut out a pattern of each.

2 Cookies: Beat all ingredients except flour in a large bowl with mixer on medium-high speed until well blended. Gradually beat in flour (dough will be soft). Divide in quarters. Pat each into a 1-in.-thick disk. Wrap individually in plastic wrap and refrigerate for at least 3 hours.

3 Heat oven to 350°F. Have baking sheet(s) ready.

4 On a lightly floured surface with a lightly floured rolling pin, roll out 1 portion dough to ¼ in. thick. (Keep remaining dough refrigerated.)

5 Flour house and triangle patterns before cutting each cookie. Place floured side down on dough. With a small, sharp knife cut around patterns. Place cut out cookies 1 in. apart on ungreased baking sheet(s). Save dough scraps.

6 Bake 10 to 12 minutes until cookies look dry but are still slightly soft. Cool on baking sheet on a wire rack 1 minute before removing to rack to cool completely. Repeat with remaining dough. Gather dough scraps and reroll only once. Cut and bake as directed above.

PER SERVING: 594 cal, 8 g pro, 72 g car, 1 g fiber, 32 g fat (12 g saturated fat), 97 mg chol, 375 mg sod

Icing & Decorations

MAKES 2½ CUPS ICING

ICING

6 Tbsp pasteurized liquid egg whites

1 lb confectioners' sugar

White, yellow, red, green and black paste or gel food colors (see Note)

DECORATIONS

Frosted Mini Chex cereal

All-Bran cereal

Tiny green circle, yellow star and red heart candy decors (see Note)

White and yellow decorating sugar (see Note)

White and red nonpareils (see Note)

Small multicolored candies (such as Nerds)

Green sprinkles (see Note)

Note: Find these ingredients in the baking section of your supermarket or in stores selling cake-decorating supplies.

1 Beat egg whites in a large bowl with mixer on high speed until frothy. Reduce speed to medium, gradually add sugar and beat 5 to 7 minutes until glossy, stiff peaks form when beaters are lifted. Keep icing covered with a damp paper towel until needed.

2 To color: For each color, put a small portion icing into a cup. Stir in food color a small amount at a time, mixing well after each addition, until desired shade. To pipe: Spoon icing into ziptop bags. Cut a tiny tip off one bottom corner.

3 To decorate: Let one color icing dry completely before spreading or piping another on top or beside the first. As a guide, use a toothpick to lightly scratch outlines of chimney, roof, door, window, etc., on surface of each house cookie. Spread white icing on roof as "snow" or as "glue" for cereal roofing and green candy decor "roof tiles." Sprinkle white sugar on plain white roof to make it sparkle. Spread white icing "snow banks" at base of houses. Spread red icing on chimney for bricks, gray for stone. When dry, pipe white icing to outline bricks and stones. Sprinkle stones with a few white nonpareils. Glue on multicolored candies for lights.

4 Spread squares and rectangles of yellow icing for windows and doors. When dry, pipe white and red icing to edge of windows and doors and decorate. Use green sprinkles for candles in windows. Pipe on trees, wreaths, swags and sleds. Add candy stars to treetops; candy hearts, nonpareils and yellow sugar to decorate swags. Let dry completely.

5 Use white icing to glue one long edge of supporting triangle cookie to back of each house so it will stand on its own. Let dry before standing cookie up.

Almond Poinsettia Cake

SERVES 16 · PREP: 45 MIN · BAKE: 25 TO 30 MIN

3/4 cup whole natural almonds, chopped

4 large eggs

1⅓ cups granulated sugar

1½ tsp baking powder

1 tsp baking soda

½ tsp salt

1 stick (½ cup) unsalted butter, melted and cooled

½ cup oil

1 tsp almond extract

3 cups all-purpose flour

1 tub (8 oz) reduced-fat sour cream

FROSTING & POINSETTIAS

1 can (8 oz) or 1 roll (7 oz) almond paste

1½ sticks (¾ cup) unsalted butter, softened

3 cups confectioners' sugar

¼ cup whole milk

½ tsp vanilla extract

¼ tsp almond extract

Yellow, red and green paste or gel food color

½ cup cherry preserves

1 Heat oven to 350°F. Grease and flour two 9-in. round cake pans. Tap out excess flour.

2 Spread almonds on baking sheet; bake 8 minutes or until toasted. Let cool. Sprinkle in prepared pans.

3 Beat eggs in a large bowl with mixer on medium-high speed until foamy. Gradually beat in sugar, then baking powder, baking soda and salt. Beat 1 minute. Beat in butter, oil and almond extract. With mixer on low speed, beat in flour in 3 additions, alternating with sour cream in 2 additions just until blended. Divide between pans; spread evenly.

4 Bake 25 to 30 minutes or until a wooden pick inserted in center of cakes comes out clean. Cool in pans on a wire rack 10 minutes. Run a knife around cakes, invert on rack and let cool completely.

5 Frosting: Finely grate 2 Tbsp almond paste (reserve remaining for poinsettias). Beat grated almond paste and butter in large bowl with mixer on medium speed until smooth. Add confectioners' sugar, milk and extracts and beat until fluffy.

6 Poinsettias (see Tip): Knead yellow food color into ½ Tbsp of remaining almond paste. Knead red color into ⅔ remaining paste, green into the rest. Place red paste on (not in) a gallon-size ziptop bag. With a rolling pin, roll out to ⅛ in. thick. Cut out petals with a pizza wheel or small knife; peel off bag. Wipe bag clean; repeat with green paste to make leaves. Roll yellow paste into tiny balls. Make markings on leaves with back of knife.

7 Place 1 cake layer, almond side down, on serving plate. Spread top with cherry preserves up to ½ in. from edge. Top with remaining cake layer, almond side down. Spread frosting over top and sides.

CAKES

8 To decorate: Arrange petals and leaves on cake to make poinsettias; glue yellow balls in centers with frosting. Refrigerate until serving. Let stand at room temperature 1 hour before serving.

PER SERVING: 594 cal, 8 g pro, 72 g car, 1 g fiber, 32 g fat (12 g saturated fat), 97 mg chol, 375 mg sod

Almond-Coconut Bundt

SERVES 16 · PREP: 30 MIN · BAKE: 30 TO 35 MIN

1½ cups (6 oz) sliced natural almonds

1¼ cups sweetened flaked coconut

1 tub (8 oz) reduced-fat sour cream

¾ cup granulated sugar

1 stick (½ cup) unsalted butter, melted

2 large eggs

1 tsp almond extract

1 tsp baking soda

½ tsp vanilla extract

1 tsp salt

1½ cups all-purpose flour

3 oz dark or bittersweet chocolate, grated on large holes of a box grater

GLAZE

3 oz dark or bittersweet chocolate

2 Tbsp stick unsalted butter

½ Tbsp light corn syrup

1 Heat oven to 350°F. Coat a 10-cup bundt pan with cooking spray. Have ready a rimmed baking sheet.

2 Spread almonds at one end of baking sheet, coconut on the other. Bake 8 to 12 minutes, stirring twice, until toasted. Cool; reserve ½ cup almonds for decoration. Finely chop remaining almonds.

3 Meanwhile, in a large bowl, whisk sour cream, sugar, butter, eggs, almond extract, baking soda, vanilla and salt until smooth. Stir in flour just until blended. Stir in coconut, chopped almonds and grated chocolate. Spread in bundt pan.

4 Bake 30 to 35 minutes until a wooden pick inserted near center of cake comes out clean. Cool in pan on a wire rack 20 minutes before inverting cake on rack to cool completely.

5 Glaze: Melt chocolate and butter; stir in corn syrup. Let cool until thick enough to spoon over top of cake. Sprinkle with reserved almond slices.

PER SERVING: 303 cal, 5 g pro, 31 g car, 3 g fiber, 19 g fat (10 g sat fat), 52 mg chol, 237 mg sod

> **Planning tip:** Can be made up to 5 days ahead. Store covered at room temperature.

Little Brandied Fruitcakes

MAKES 12 · PREP: 35 MIN (NOT INCLUDING SOAKING FRUIT) · BAKE: 30 TO 35 MIN

3 cups chopped candied fruit, a mix of orange and lemon peels, cherries and pineapple and/or other dried fruit (such as apricots, raisins or cranberries)

¾ cup brandy or dark rum

2 sticks (1 cup) unsalted butter, softened

1 cup packed brown sugar

½ tsp ground cinnamon

½ tsp baking soda

¼ tsp each ground cloves and nutmeg

2 large eggs

¼ cup milk

2 cups all-purpose flour

1½ cups pecans, coarsely chopped

ICING

2 cups confectioners' sugar

3 to 4 Tbsp milk

1½ cups chopped candied or dried fruit

> **Storage tip:** Store undecorated cakes airtight at room temperature for 1 week, or in the freezer for 3 months.

1 Cover fruit with ½ cup brandy. Soak 24 hours at room temperature.

2 Heat oven to 325°F. Generously grease and flour two mini-Bundt pans with six 1-cup-capacity cups in each (see Note).

3 In a large bowl, beat butter, brown sugar, cinnamon, baking soda, cloves and nutmeg with mixer until well blended. Beat in eggs and milk. On low speed, beat in flour until just blended. Stir in fruit along with any liquid and pecans. Spoon about ½ cup into each mini-Bundt pan, smoothing tops.

4 Bake 30 to 35 minutes or until a wooden pick inserted in middle of cakes comes out clean. Cool on wire rack 15 to 20 minutes, then invert and rap pan down sharply to release cakes. Spoon 1 tsp brandy over top of each. Cool completely.

5 Icing: Beat confectioners' sugar and milk until well blended. Drizzle over tops of cakes. Sprinkle with chopped fruit. Let icing set. You can decorate up to two days before serving or giving, but make sure to store airtight.

PER FRUITCAKE: 712 cal, 5 g pro, 114 g car, 3 g fiber, 27 g fat (11 g sat fat), 76 mg chol, 250 mg sod

> **Note:** NordicWare sells Bundtlette pans at gourmet shops, baking supply stores and online at www.nordicware.com.

Peppermint Cream Puff Ring

SERVES 12 · PREP & CHILL: ABOUT 5 HR · BAKE: 40 TO 45 MIN

About 1⅓ cups heavy (whipping) cream

1 cup loosely packed mint leaves (about 40)

PASTRY

½ cup each whole milk and water

1 stick (½ cup) unsalted butter, cut in 8 pieces

1 Tbsp granulated sugar

¼ tsp salt

1 cup all-purpose flour

4 large eggs

CREAM FILLING

¼ cup plus 2 Tbsp granulated sugar

½ cup cold crème fraîche or sour cream

GLAZE

2 oz bittersweet chocolate, chopped

1 Tbsp heavy (whipping) cream

1 Tbsp light corn syrup

3 Tbsp toasted sliced almonds

PER SERVING: 329 cal, 5 g pro, 22 g car, 1 g fiber, 25 g fat (15 g sat fat), 139 mg chol, 100 mg sod

1 Bring 1⅓ cups cream and the mint leaves to a boil. Remove from heat, cover and steep 1 hour. Pour into a bowl; refrigerate until cold, about 3 hours or overnight.

2 Heat oven to 425°F. Line a baking sheet with parchment paper and have ready 1 gallon-size ziptop bag and a pastry bag fitted with a large star piping tip. Draw an 8-in. circle on the parchment paper; turn paper over.

3 Pastry: Bring milk, water, butter, sugar and salt to boil in a medium saucepan over medium-high heat. Add flour all at once; stir energetically with a wooden spoon until dough comes together in a shiny mass (bottom of pan will be covered with a thin film of flour). Cook, stirring constantly, 1 to 2 minutes. Transfer hot dough to a large bowl.

4 Using a sturdy mixer, beat in eggs, 1 at a time, until each is blended (dough will be thick and shiny). Spoon warm dough into a ziptop bag; cut ¾ in. off 1 corner.

5 Pipe a ring about 1 in. thick on circle on parchment paper. Pipe a second ring inside first, just touching first ring. Pipe a third ring on top where rings meet. (If there's extra dough, pipe mounds for cream puffs or strips for eclairs.)

6 Bake 20 minutes, reduce oven temperature to 375°F and bake 20 to 25 minutes more until puffed, brown and firm. Transfer sheet to a wire rack; let ring cool completely. (Ring will sink; that's OK.)

7 Cream Filling: Strain peppermint cream into a measuring cup, adding more chilled heavy cream if needed to make 1⅓ cups. Pour into a large bowl, add ¼ cup sugar and beat with mixer on medium speed until stiff peaks form when beaters are lifted. Stir remaining 2 Tbsp sugar into crème fraîche; gently fold into whipped cream.

8 Using a serrated knife and gentle sawing motion, slice top off pastry ring. Pull out and discard soft dough inside base. Carefully transfer base to a serving platter.

9 Spoon cream filling into prepared pastry bag. Pipe large rosettes close together into base. Pipe another row of rosettes on first row, piping top rosettes between bottom rosettes. Add pastry top. Refrigerate while making Glaze.

10 Glaze: Microwave chocolate, cream and corn syrup in small bowl on high, stirring every 10 seconds until chocolate melts and glaze is smooth. Spread on top of pastry ring; sprinkle with almonds. Refrigerate at least 1 hour, or up to 8 hours before serving.

Mocha Cappuccino Cake

SERVES 16 · PREP: 45 MIN · BAKE: 1 HR

CAKE

1½ sticks (¾ cup) unsalted butter, softened

1¼ cups granulated sugar

2 tsp baking powder

1 tsp baking soda

½ tsp salt

3 large eggs

2 tsp vanilla extract

3 cups all-purpose flour

1½ cups reduced-fat sour cream

¼ cup semisweet mini chocolate chips

¼ cup packed light-brown sugar

1 tsp each *instant coffee powder and ground cinnamon*

FROSTING

1½ tsp instant coffee powder

¾ tsp vanilla extract

6 oz cream cheese, softened

¾ stick (6 Tbsp) unsalted butter, softened

½ tsp ground cinnamon

3 cups confectioners' sugar

Decoration: *chocolate-covered coffee beans and unsweetened cocoa powder*

PER SERVING: 471 cal, 6 g pro, 63 g car, 1 g fiber, 22 g fat (13 g saturated fat), 94 mg chol, 402 mg sod

1 Heat oven to 350°F. Grease and flour a 10-in. tube pan with a removable bottom.

2 Cake: In a large bowl with mixer on low speed, beat butter, sugar, baking powder, baking soda and salt until creamy. Increase speed to medium; beat 2 minutes or until pale and fluffy. Beat in eggs, 1 at a time, until well blended. Beat in vanilla. Reduce speed to low; beat in flour in 3 additions, alternating with sour cream in 2 additions, beating just until blended.

3 In a medium bowl, combine chocolate chips, brown sugar, coffee powder and cinnamon. Add 1 cup batter; stir until blended. Spoon 3 cups plain batter into prepared pan, spreading evenly. Spoon a ring of brown sugar batter ¾ in. from center and sides of pan over plain batter. Top with spoonfuls of remaining plain batter. Spread gently to cover brown sugar batter.

4 Bake 1 hour or until a wooden pick inserted in center of cake comes out clean (cake will have risen only halfway up pan). Cool in pan on a wire rack.

5 Frosting: Stir coffee powder and vanilla in a large bowl until coffee dissolves. Add cream cheese, butter and cinnamon. Beat with mixer on medium speed until fluffy. Beat in confectioners' sugar, 1 cup at a time until smooth.

6 Run a knife around pan side and remove. Invert cake onto a serving plate; run a knife around pan bottom and remove. Frost cake.

7 To decorate: Cut an 8½-in. round out of sturdy paper; cut assorted-size stars out of the paper. Place paper with cut-outs on cake, sift cocoa powder over cake, then carefully lift off paper. Place chocolate-covered coffee beans around cake.

CAKES

Nutty Caramel Acorns

MAKES 46 · PREP & DIP: 1 HR · BAKE: 14 MIN PER BATCH

1 stick (½ cup) light or regular unsalted butter, softened

⅓ cup packed dark-brown sugar

2 large egg yolks

1 cup chopped nuts (black walnuts, cashews, peanuts or your favorite)

1½ tsp vanilla extract

½ tsp baking powder

¼ tsp salt

1¾ cups all-purpose flour

½ cup chocolate sprinkles (jimmies)

1 pkg (14 oz) classic caramels, unwrapped

1½ Tbsp water

Storage tip: Store airtight at cool room temperature with wax paper between layers up to 1 week.

1 Heat oven to 350°F. You'll need a baking sheet(s).

2 Beat butter, sugar and yolks in a large bowl with mixer on medium speed until fluffy. Beat in ½ cup of the nuts, the vanilla, baking powder and salt. With mixer on low speed, gradually beat in flour until a soft dough forms.

3 Roll rounded teaspoons of dough into balls. Shape as acorns with a pointed top. Place point up, 1 in. apart, on ungreased baking sheet(s). Bake 14 minutes, until bottoms are golden brown. Cool on rack.

4 Place remaining ½ cup nuts and the sprinkles in food processor; pulse until finely chopped. Mound mixture on a sheet of wax paper. Melt caramels and water in a bowl in microwave as package directs.

5 Dunk acorn cookies into caramel 1 at a time, turning with a fork to coat. Lift and scrape excess caramel from bottom against top edge of bowl. Use a second fork to scrape acorn from first fork onto nut mixture to coat bottoms. Transfer to a wax paper-lined cookie sheet and refrigerate to set caramel. Reheat caramel in microwave to keep it fluid while dipping remaining acorns.

PER ACORN: 89 cal, 2 g pro, 13 g car, 0 g fiber, 4 g fat (1 g sat fat), 12 mg chol, 51 mg sod

Pecan Tassies

MAKES 48 · PREP & CHILL: ABOUT 1¼ HR · BAKE: 20 MIN PER BATCH

2 sticks (1 cup) unsalted butter, softened

6 oz cream cheese, at room temperature

2 cups all-purpose flour

FILLING

3 large eggs, slightly beaten

1¾ cups packed brown sugar

3 Tbsp unsalted stick butter, softened or melted

¾ tsp vanilla extract

¼ tsp salt

1 cup pecans, coarsely chopped

Decoration: confectioners' sugar

1 Beat butter and cream cheese in a large bowl with mixer on medium speed until well combined. Beat in flour until just blended. Shape dough into a 1-in.-thick disk, wrap and refrigerate at least 30 minutes until firm.

2 Heat oven to 375°F. Have ungreased miniature muffin pan(s) ready. (Mini muffin cups measure 1¼ in. across bottom.)

3 Divide dough in quarters. Roll each portion into a 6-in.-long log. Cut 1 log in 12 equal pieces. With floured hands, flatten each piece to a 3-in. round and fit into a muffin cup (dough will extend above the cup).

4 Filling: Beat first 5 ingredients until well mixed. Spoon 2 tsp into each muffin cup; top with pecans.

5 Bake 20 minutes or until pastry is brown and filling is set. Cool briefly in pan on a wire rack, then carefully remove cups, loosening them with tip of a knife if needed. Place on rack to cool completely. Repeat with remaining dough and filling. Dust tassies with confectioners' sugar.

PER TASSIE: 124 cal, 1 g pro, 13 g car, 0 g fiber, 8 g fat (4 g sat fat), 29 mg chol, 30 mg sod

Chocolate-Pecan Tassies

MAKES 20 · PREP & CHILL: ABOUT 2½ HR · BAKE: 27 TO 30 MIN

1 stick (½ cup) unsalted butter, softened

1 brick (3 oz) cream cheese, at room temperature

1 cup plus 2 Tbsp all-purpose flour

¼ tsp salt

FILLING

1 oz unsweetened baking chocolate

1½ Tbsp unsalted butter

⅔ cup packed brown sugar

1 large egg

2 tsp vanilla extract

½ cup finely chopped unsalted dry roasted peanuts

2 oz semisweet baking chocolate

PER TASSIE: 163 cal, 3 g pro, 16 g car, 1 g fiber, 11 g fat (6 g sat fat), 30 mg chol, 49 mg sod

Storage tip: Store airtight at room temperature in a single layer up to 1 week, or freeze up to 2 months.

1 Beat butter and cream cheese in a large bowl with mixer on medium speed to blend. On low speed, beat in flour and salt to combine. Refrigerate covered 1 hour or until firm.

2 Place oven rack in lowest position; heat to 350°F. Have ungreased miniature muffin pan(s) ready.

3 **Filling:** Microwave chocolate and butter in a medium bowl 1 to 2 minutes. Stir until smooth. Stir in sugar, egg and vanilla, then peanuts until combined.

4 Roll level tablespoons dough into 20 balls. With floured fingers, press a ball over bottom and up sides of each ungreased muffin cup, extending slightly above rim. Fill each ¾ full with filling.

5 Bake 27 to 30 minutes until edges are lightly browned (tops will crack slightly). Cool in pan on a wire rack 15 minutes. Invert pan; tap to loosen tassies onto rack; turn upright and cool completely.

6 Melt semisweet chocolate as package directs. Scrape into a ziptop bag. Cut tip off corner and drizzle chocolate over tassies. Let chocolate set at least 30 minutes.

Square Ginger Truffles

2 bars (4 oz each) bittersweet chocolate, chopped

⅓ cup plus 2 tsp heavy (whipping) cream

⅓ cup finely chopped crystallized ginger

2 Tbsp cognac or other very good brandy

½ tsp vanilla extract

Decoration: plain or tinted confectioners' sugar (see Note 1), unsweetened cocoa powder or chocolate coating (see Note 2)

Note 1: To tint confectioners' sugar, place ⅓ cup in a small ziptop bag. Add 10 drops food color. Knead until sugar is colored.

Note 2: To cover with chocolate coating, place a wire rack on a baking sheet lined with wax paper. Chop 2 bars (4 oz each) bittersweet chocolate. Melt in a saucepan over low heat, or in microwave on high, stirring at 10-second intervals, until smooth. Cool to just above room temperature. Rest a truffle on a fork; lower into chocolate to coat. Lift from chocolate; let excess drip off. Place on wire rack. Refrigerate until set.

1 Line an 8-in. square baking pan with nonstick foil, letting foil extend 2 in. above pan on opposite sides.

2 Stir chocolate and cream in a small saucepan over low heat, or in a microwave on high, stirring at 10-second intervals, until chocolate melts and mixture is smooth. Remove from heat.

3 Stir in ginger, cognac and vanilla until blended. Pour into prepared pan; spread evenly. Cover and refrigerate at least 2 hours until set.

4 Lift foil from pan. Remove from foil to a cutting board. Cut with a sharp knife in 6 rows lengthwise and 6 crosswise. Sift confectioners' sugar or cocoa over tops, or dip in chocolate coating.

PER TRUFFLE: 47 cal, 0 g pro, 5 g car, 0 g fiber, 3 g fat (1 g sat fat), 3 mg chol, 2 mg sod

ORANGE-HAZELNUT TRUFFLES

Prepare through Step 2. In Step 3, omit ginger, cognac and vanilla; stir in 2 Tbsp orange liqueur and 1 Tbsp grated orange zest. Proceed as directed. Coat truffles with melted chocolate; sprinkle with chopped toasted hazelnuts.

PER TRUFFLE: 75 cal, 1 g pro, 7 g car, 1 g fiber, 5 g fat (3 g sat fat), 3 mg chol, 2 mg sod

MOCHA TRUFFLES

Stir 1 Tbsp instant coffee granules into the heavy cream. Prepare through Step 2. In Step 3, omit ginger, cognac and vanilla; stir in 2 Tbsp coffee liqueur. Proceed as directed. Sift cocoa powder over top.

PER TRUFFLE: 44 cal, 1 g pro, 4 g car, 1 g fiber, 3 g fat (2 g sat fat), 3 mg chol, 2 mg sod

Candy Cane Toffee

MAKES 2¼ LB · PREP & CHILL: 2¼ HR

1½ cups granulated sugar

2 sticks (1 cup) unsalted butter

3 Tbsp water

1 Tbsp light corn syrup

1 tsp vanilla extract

2 cups semisweet chocolate chips

¾ cup coarsely chopped peppermint candy canes

Storage tip: This brittle can be stored in a refrigerator (or airtight at room temperature) for one month.

1 Line a 13 x 9-in. baking pan with foil, letting foil extend about 2 in. above opposite ends of pan. Lightly coat foil with cooking spray.

2 In a heavy-bottomed medium saucepan over medium heat, bring sugar, butter, water and corn syrup to a boil. Boil without stirring until a candy thermometer registers 300 to 310°F. (Or, drop a small amount into ice water. When mixture forms a brittle mass that snaps easily when pressed between fingers, it's ready.) Off heat, stir in vanilla (be careful, it splatters).

3 Pour into prepared pan. Wait 2 minutes, then sprinkle evenly with chocolate chips. When chips become shiny, spread over toffee. Sprinkle with chopped candy cane.

4 Refrigerate at least 2 hours until cold. Lift foil by ends onto a cutting board; break toffee in bite-size pieces.

PER SERVING: 135 cal, 0 g pro, 17 g car, 1 g fiber, 8 g fat (5 g sat fat), 13 mg chol, 37 mg sod

Table of Equivalents

ABBREVIATIONS

Teaspoon: tsp
Tablespoon: Tbsp

U.S.	METRIC
ounce = oz	milliliter = ml
pint = pt	liter = l
pound = lb	gram = g
quart = qt	kilogram = kg
inch = in.	millimeter = mm
foot = ft	centimeter = cm

VOLUME

U.S.	METRIC
¼ tsp	1 ml
½ tsp	2.5 ml
¾ tsp	4 ml
1 tsp	5 ml
1¼ tsp	6 ml
1½ tsp	7.5 ml
1¾ tsp	8.5 ml
2 tsp	10 ml
1 Tbsp	15 ml
2 Tbsp	30 ml
¼ cup	60 ml
⅓ cup	80 ml
½ cup	120 ml
⅔ cup	160 ml
¾ cup	180 ml
1 cup	240 ml
1½ cups	355 ml
2 cups (1 pint)	475 ml
3 cups	710 ml
4 cups (1 quart)	.95 l
1.06 quart	1 l
4 quarts (1 gallon)	3.8 l

WEIGHTS

U.S.	METRIC
.035 oz	1 g
¼ oz	7 g
½ oz	14 g
¾ oz	21 g
1 oz	28 g
1½ oz	42.5 g
2 oz	57 g
3 oz	85 g
4 oz	113 g
5 oz	142 g
6 oz	170 g
7 oz	198 g
8 oz (½ lb)	227 g
10 oz	315 g
12 oz (¾ lb)	375 g
14 oz	440 g
16 oz (1 lb)	454 g
2.2 lbs	1 kg

OVEN TEMPERATURES

FAHRENHEIT	CELSIUS	GAS
250	120	½
275	140	1
300	150	2
325	160	3
350	180	4
375	190	5
400	200	6
425	220	7
450	230	8
475	240	9
500	260	10

WHEN A RECIPE CALLS FOR	A DIGITAL PRINTOUT WILL READ
4 oz (¼ lb)	.25 lb
8 oz (½ lb)	.50 lb
12 oz (¾ lb)	.75 lb
1 lb (16 oz)	1.00 lb
1 lb 4 oz (1¼ lb)	1.25 lb

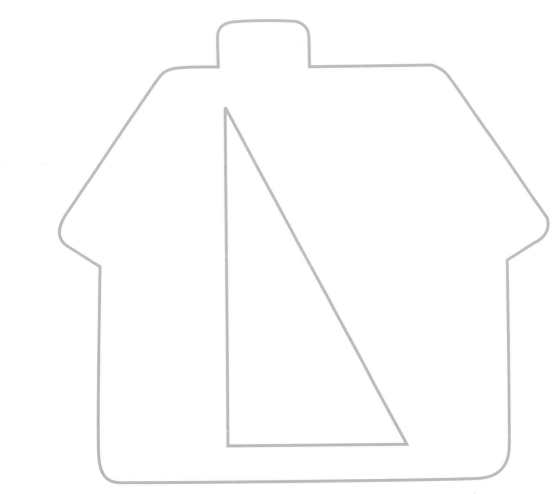

"Stand-Up Gingerbread House" and supporting triangle outline (recipe page 74)

Photo Credits

Pages 6, 9, 10: Jacqueline Hopkins; pp. 13, 15: Alan Richardson; pp. 16, 19: Dasha Wright; p. 21: Charles Schiller; p. 23: Dasha Wright; pp. 24-25: Erik Rank; p. 27: Alan Richardson; p. 28: Charles Schiller; p. 30: Erik Rank; pp. 32, 34: Jacqueline Hopkins; pp. 37, 38: Dasha Wright; p. 42: Alan Richardson; pp. 43, 44: Dasha Wright; p. 46: Erik Rank; pp. 48, 51, 52: Jacqueline Hopkins; p. 54: Dasha Wright; p. 57: Anastasios Mentis; p. 59: Jacqueline Hopkins; p. 61: Erik Rank; p. 62: Alan Richardson; p. 64: Jacqueline Hopkins; p. 67: John Uher; p. 69: Jacqueline Hopkins; pp. 71, 72: Sang An; p. 75: Tom McWilliam; p. 77: Charles Schiller; pp. 78, 80: Jacqueline Hopkins; p. 83: Anastasios Mentis; p. 85: Jacqueline Hopkins; p. 86: Kate Sears; p. 88: Alan Richardson; p. 89: Charles Schiller; pp. 90, 93: Jacqueline Hopkins.

Recipes appearing on pages 24, 25, 30, 46 and 61: Courtesy of Wilton.

First published in 2008 in the
United States of America by
Filipacchi Publishing
1633 Broadway
New York, NY 10019

Woman's Day is a registered trademark of Hachette Filipacchi Media U.S., Inc.

Design: Patricia Fabricant
Copyediting: Jennifer Ladonne
Production: Ed Barredo

ISBN 10: 1-933231-43-2
ISBN 13: 978-1-933231-43-3

Library of Congress Control Number: 2008924233

Printed in China